THE ANATOMY OF THE CAT

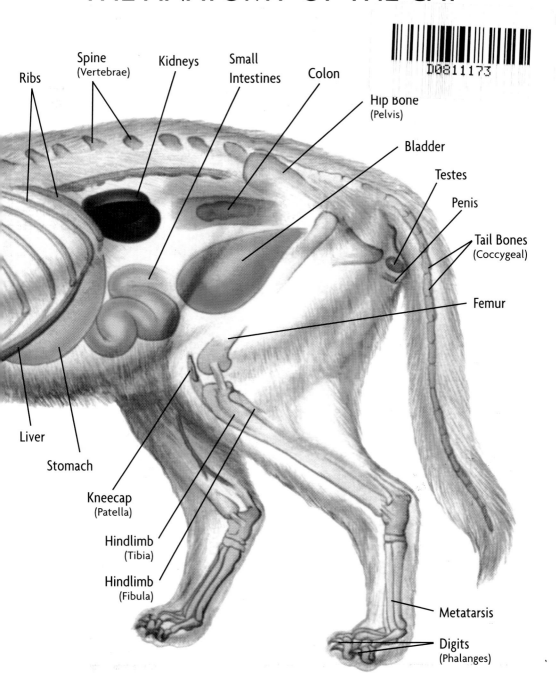

Ribs

Spine
(Vertebrae)

Kidneys

Small
Intestines

Colon

Hip Bone
(Pelvis)

Bladder

Testes

Penis

Tail Bones
(Coccygeal)

Femur

Liver

Stomach

Kneecap
(Patella)

Hindlimb
(Tibia)

Hindlimb
(Fibula)

Metatarsis

Digits
(Phalanges)

Birman Cat

◇

By Dennis Kelsey-Wood

Birman Cat

Contents

PUBLISHED IN THE UNITED KINGDOM BY:

INTERPET
PUBLISHING

Vincent Lane, Dorking   Surrey RH4 3YX   England

ISBN 1-84286-038-0

PHOTO CREDITS:
Michael W Brim, Cat Fanciers' Association, Carolina Biological Supply,
Cheryl Ertelt, Fleabusters Rx for Fleas, Isabelle Français,
James R Hayden, Interpet, Dwight R Kuhn, Dr Dennis Kunkel,
Phototake, RPB, Jean Claude Revy,
W B Saunders Company and Erin Winters.

The publisher wishes to thank
Gerbipur Cattery, K A and L M Gerke, P Lloyd, M Stiner
and the rest of the owners of cats featured in this book.

Mythical and mysterious, the Sacred Cat of Burma delivers romance and companionship to modern-day cat lovers.

When a cat breed is surrounded with a myth or legend–especially one that has a believable ring to it–the breed receives special attention. If its origins also involve a web of mystery and intrigue, this creates further interest. Its possibly less romantic origins can then be quietly forgotten and become the famed skeletons hidden away in the cupboard of the past. With the Birman you get both a myth and a mystery that to this day have been neither proved nor disproved.

THE MYTH OF THE BIRMAN
The myth of the Sacred Cat of Burma takes us back many centuries ago near Lake Incaougji in Indo-China. There amongst the pagodas was to be found the temple of Lao-Tsun. It housed the blue-eyed golden statue of the goddess Tsun-Kyan-Kse who was responsible for presiding over the souls of priests when they died. On such occasions, the soul of a priest would enter the body of one of the hundred longhaired golden-eyed white cats that lived in the temple. When the cat died, the priest's soul would be released to

complete its ethereal journey to paradise.

The head priest was called Mun-Ha and he had a faithful white cat called Sinh. One night while the holy man meditated in front of the golden goddess, the temple was attacked and Mun-Ha died. At the moment of his death, Sinh stood on his body and gazed into the eyes of the goddess. His eye colour changed to a sapphire blue while his fur turned golden. His bodily extremities became dark brown like the rich soil of the land. But where his paws rested on his master's body, the fur remained white as a symbol of the cat's purity. The soul of Mun-Ha passed into the body of Sinh.

On witnessing this, all the other priests rallied and drove the attackers from the temple. They then formed a circle around Sinh to seek his guidance as to who should be the new high priest. Sinh turned and stared at a young priest called Ligoa who was thus the chosen one. By the next day the remaining ninety-nine white temple cats had also changed colour to match those of Sinh. During the next seven days Sinh refused all food and water. He died peacefully on the seventh day. His spirit and the soul of his master journeyed to their heavenly paradise to be embraced by the great god Song-Hio.

There are in fact numerous variations on the myth as described here, but all relate the same basic story. The notion of human souls passing into the body of a cat is not unique. In Far Eastern religions, similar myths are told, though not with quite the same poignant storyline as that of Mun-Ha and Sinh.

THE MYSTERY

The mystery of the origins of the Birman is an extension of the myth and involves two gentlemen. One is an Englishman, Russell Gordon, variably cited as being the Honourable, Sir or Major. He was said to have been a serving officer in the British army in India. The second person is a Frenchman called Auguste Pavie, said to have been an explorer of the region.

It appears that in either 1898 or 1916 the worshippers of Tsun-Kyan-Kse were again in trouble and their temple was under threat. The two gentlemen came to the aid of the monks and helped them relocate to a new temple in Tibet. In appreciation of their help, the priests sent them, in 1918, a pair of these rare and highly regarded felines. The cats were shipped to France, where it was said that both Gordon and Pavie then lived. But on the journey the male died, though his companion, Sita, who was a kitten, survived.

Another story states that a Mr Vanderbilt, an American million-

aire, paid an unscrupulous temple worker to steal a pair of the cats. These were then transported on Vanderbilt's yacht to Nice in France, arriving in 1918. In 1925, in a thesis on cat breeds, which included the Birman, a vet, Phillippe Jumaud, mentions Vanderbilt. This may be the source of that particular story. In an article of that same year, he also mentions a lady, Mme Leotardi, as being a Birman breeder of some experience.

In 1926 the same author states that a Mme Thadde-Hadish was the importer of the original pair of cats (thus contradicting the other story that the male had died during the trip). More notably she was the owner of a Sita daughter called Poupee de Madalpour. This cat eventually became the property of Mme Leotardi. Jamaud's comments certainly add influential weight to the belief that the breed originated in Burma. However, he may only have been passing on information he had been given, which he had no reason to disbelieve.

THOUGHTS ON THE ORIGINS

Were cats of the Birman type in existence in Burma (now called Myanmar) during the turn of the century years, it would seem highly likely that they would have been brought to Europe by the then ruling British. The Siamese had made its appearance as early

TRUTH IN THE MYTH?

As enchanting as it is, the myth of the Birman does not stand up to any serious investigation. But, hypothetically, if it were based on truth, then the Birman would more correctly be the Sacred Cat of India or China! As for the mysterious Russell Gordon and Auguste Pavie, nothing seems to be known of them.

Many hobby experts have attempted to trace these 'Indiana Jones'-style adventurers who rescued priests and cats from their 'Temple of Doom', but no one has succeeded. The dates, the goddess and the events quoted cannot be matched to any known historic situations of that period. Likewise, there is no further information to be found on Mr Vanderbilt.

as 1871 at the first cat show in London. Cat shows were organised in Paris (and elsewhere in France) from 1890 yet, based on present knowledge, the beautiful Birman did not appear at a show until 1926.

There are thus many problems in the popular version of the Birman's history. More than a few experts believe it was all contrived to give the developing breed a fascinating myth accompanied by a credible history. This would give it extra appeal at a time when the cat fancy was attracting new enthusi-

The Turkish Angora has been linked to the creation of many longhaired breeds, including the Birman.

Around her the storyline was then developed. Certainly there is ample scope for much more research into this fascinating subject. This may yield some vital information that will clarify certain aspects of the breed's history.

However, one fact will not change. The breed cannot claim any pure line of descent. Other breeds were involved in creating the beautiful cat that bears the name of Birman. These breeds included the Persian, the Angora, and especially the Siamese. A few long- and shorthaired cats of

The Persian, with its luxuriant, dense coat, may be a distant relation to the Birman.

asts and when competition to establish new breeds was strong.

It is always possible that a cat marked like the Birman did arrive in France from Burma or Thailand. But it is also possible the breed was developed in the area of Nice from a cat called Sita.

unknown type were also involved. It must be added that the Siamese of past years was nothing like the svelte cat of today. It was much more powerfully built and had more dense fur.

A mordern-day Siamese showing off its svelte build, quite unlike its ancestors that may have contributed to the Birman's origin.

DOCUMENTED EARLY HISTORY
What is known for sure is that the Birman was developed in France, and it all started with the cat Sita. She was mated to Madalpour, who

The 'white glove' mystery: how many Birmans can be traced to the original cat Sita from France, and further to the mythical cat Sinh.

was born in November 1918. Nothing more appears to be known about him. Their union produced, among others, a female called Poupee de Madalpour. She was to become very famous and one of the important models on which the breed would develop.

However, due to the lack of information from the early 1920s and 1930s, it is difficult to judge just how important she was from a breeding perspective. The lack of pedigrees at that period means there is little evidence to link her directly to other cats that would eventually be the root stock of the emerging breed.

It is now appropriate to make important comments. During the developmental years of the Birman, matings were effected that were not recorded on pedigrees. Information was passed by word of mouth. This means we know little of what took place. Birmans of unknown origin are documented for many years after the breed was well established, indeed into the 1970s. This does not necessarily mean they were not Birmans, though clearly many were not. They may have been unregistered Birmans without a pedigree. Some of these were then given names and were registered as the breed started to gain in popularity and as pedigrees became more widely used.

In the years that followed 1919, the Birman steadily gained devotees. During this period the two major catteries were those of Mlle Marcelle Adam (Madalpour) and Mlle Boyer (Kaabaa). To a very large extent, the Birman breed was developed from their stock. The breeding lines of all other catteries of the day (and to this day) can be traced to these. However, the Birman was also being developed in Germany.

The catteries of Von Alsen, Adschemi and Fronhau appear in numerous early pedigrees. Their lines were later fused with those of the major French catteries. In 1925 the Birman was given breed status with its own standard in the Federation Feline Française (FFF). The President of that association was Mlle Marcelle Adam.

THE YEARS 1926–1945
From the evidence of photographs, cats such as Dieu d'Arakan, born of unknown parents in 1930, were excellent examples of the breed. In contrast, Manou de Madalpour, a Poupee son, was much less striking. He was indicative of the wide breed variation within that time period. Important cats of these early years were to have a lasting effect on the breed. These included Fly de Kaabaa and Youla de Madalpour, both born in 1928, and Youla de Kaabaa, born in 1938. Interestingly, Youla de Kaabaa's parents were Kiou, who was a gloved Siamese, and Tai, who was a non-gloved Birman.

Fly was one of the most influential cats of the time and was bred many times to his numerous daughters. As is quite normal when a breed is being developed from a limited gene pool, the level of inbreeding in the early years was quite intense. It became steadily less so as the Birman population increased. During this period there were also black, white, bicolour, blue and cream 'Birmans' as well as numerous Siamese and their hybrids within the breeding nucleus.

A grandson of Fly was Orloff

Although
practised on
occasion,
inbreeding is
uncommon in
most breeding
programmes
today.

A BIRMAN BY ANY OTHER NAME...

The breed's present name of Birman is taken from the French name for it, Birmanie. When the breed was written about in Britain years ago, its name was spelled 'Burman'. It was also known in its earliest years as the Burmese Sacred Cat. This caused some confusion during the 1930s when the Burmese breed *(pictured below)* was itself being developed. The two breeds are totally unrelated.

The present-day Birman is a monument to the diligence, determination and foresight of breeders in France and Germany. They made whatever sacrifices were needed to ensure the breed survived a World War so that breeders and devotees of today could enjoy the pleasure of owning one or more of these true feline jewels.

de Kaabaa, born in 1943. He was to have an enormous influence on the breed as a consequence of chance. Just when things seemed to be going nicely for the breed, the Second World War commenced. It had a catastrophic effect on the Birman. Many fine examples perished and many catteries were wiped out.

By the end of the war, it was thought that only one or two Birmans had survived. Fortunately, while the number was very low, it was higher than originally thought.

Even the German lines mentioned survived the ravages and were rebuilt in the late 1940s. Breeding did not come to an end in the war years. A few Birmans born during this period were able to pass on the genes of the numerous earlier breed pillars.

THE MODERN ERA

It was during the 1950s that the Birman really began to re-establish itself. Once again the Madalpour and Kaabaa catteries were to be the dominant lines. There were many fine cats, and a few can be mentioned that were to have an enormous influence on the breed throughout the world. One was Orloff, already mentioned. His chance to be a major force was a consequence of his surviving the war. Amongst his many offspring was Xenia de Kaabaa, who proved a very influential female. Mated to her father, she produced Yougi in 1951. He became a true breed pillar.

Of the many cats that carried his genes were Hamlet de Madalpour (1957) and numerous cats of the du Clos Fleuri line, which was to become an important cattery. One cat that became a dominant force in America and elsewhere was Korrigan de la Regnarderie, bred by Mme Lavoinne in France during 1961. He carried both Kaabaa and Madalpour lines. When imported to America, his name was changed to Korrigan of Clover Creek. He is seen on many American pedigrees of the 1960s, as well as those in England, mainland Europe and elsewhere.

During this early post-war period, there are a number of especially famous cattery names (used as a suffix or prefix) that will be variably found on any Birman's ancestral pedigree. These are Assindia, Alsen and Adschemi, (Germany); Lugh, Khlaramour, Clos Fleuri, Crespieres, Ormailly and Muses (France). Of course, Kaabaa and Madalpour of France are the most famous.

THE BIRMAN IN BRITAIN

Although British fanciers had known about the Birman for many years (it was illustrated and described in a British cat book at least as early as 1961), it

THE 1926 PARIS SHOW

Two significant days in the development of the Birman breed were the 14th and 15th of November 1926. This is when an international show was held in Paris at which three Birmans were exhibited. Poupee de Madalpour attracted particular attention. One comment stated she was owned by Madame Leotardi and was a particularly outstanding example, displaying all of the characteristics of this rare breed.

When Poupee was mated to a Siamese (described as Laotian Lynx Cat), she produced, amongst others, Ijadi-Tsun de Kaabaa, one of the first of Mlle Boyer's Kaabaa Birmans. In the years that followed this show, interest in the Birman grew steadily.

was not until 1965 that the breed was imported. During that year Elsie Fisher and Margaret Richards attended a cat show in Paris. There they saw a beautiful blue kitten of the de Lugh line of Mme Yvonne Drossier. They were totally smitten. Later that year they formed a partnership under the prefix of Paranjoti and imported three Birmans. These were a seal point, Nouky De Mon Reve, and two blue points, Osaka de Lugh and Orlamonde de Khlaramour. In the following year, Elizabeth Towe widened the gene pool by importing Pipo du Clos Fleuri.

Birmans in Britain today are exhibited in the Semi-Longhair category.

The Birman shows off its seal lynx point coloration.

The Birman proved to be highly popular and a most welcome addition to the longhaired breeds. However, in shows it was at some disadvantage because it was grouped with the Persian and was often regarded as 'a second-class citizen' to that breed.

During 1967 Elsie Fisher reverted to her own prefix of Praha and imported Ghandi von Assindia, a fine blue male. His great-grandfather was the famous Korrigan of Clover Creek. Margaret Richards also reverted to her own prefix of Smokeyhill. In the following years both breeders enjoyed enormous success, producing many Champions, Grand Champions and International Champions. Their lines are seen in those of breeders all over the world.

The original imports already named represented the combined genes of the best Birmans of the day. Indeed, their pedigrees read like a 'who's who' of the great catteries of both France and Germany. The breed gained official recognition in Britain in 1966. One year later it gained similar status in America, where it had first been imported in 1959. In 1993 the breed was regrouped in Britain for show purposes into a new category called Semi-Longhair cats.

A Portrait of the

BIRMAN CAT

Superficially, the Birman could be mistaken by the uninitiated for a Colourpoint Persian with the addition of white feet. However, in its conformation it is rather different, especially in respect of its head. A better comparison would be with the mitted variety of the Ragdoll breed. This was developed in the 1960s, using the Birman in its programme. Until the arrival of the Ragdoll, the Birman was unique in the cat world for its colour pattern.

Possessed of a wonderful temperament, the Birman is a powerfully built cat, yet one that imparts a serene appearance. It is neither svelte nor cobby. Its standard of points varies little around the world and is based on that originally prepared for it in France during 1925.

A standard is a written blueprint of what a good example should look like. It can only ever be a broad guide because all members of a breed will vary somewhat in their appearance. The only way to appreciate how a standard should be interpreted at any given moment in time is to visit a major cat show and study the winners. These represent an accredited breed judge's opinion of the cats, and how they compare to the standard.

The following description, while not an official standard, is based on reference to these. It should meet the needs of most hobbyists. Potential breeders and exhibitors should obtain the official Birman standard of the association with which they intend to register their cat(s).

Head: The skull is round and broad. In profile the nose shows a slight curve, called a Roman nose in some standards. There is no noticeable 'stop,' meaning an indentation where the forehead meets the nose. The cheeks are round and full, the chin well

The Birman's head is round and broad, without a noticeable 'stop'.

Tail: Of medium length, the tail should appear proportionate to the body, meaning neither too long nor too short.

Coat: This is long. Its texture is silky, this being conducive to the minimum of mats. The hairs may curl slightly on the belly.

Eyes of the Birman should blend with the face to give the cat its distinctive sweet expression.

developed. The nose should form a perpendicular line with the lower jaw, which allows for the correct incisor bite.

Ears: Of medium length and set well apart, the ears have a rounded tip.

Eyes: These are almost round. They should never be bold, but should blend with the face to create a sweet expression. Their colour is blue, the deeper the better.

Body: Long and massive. However, length should not be such that it makes the legs appear too short.

Legs and Paws: Of medium length, the legs are of good thickness. The paws are short, round and firm. There should be five toes on the front feet, four on the rear.

Birmans are large, athletic cats with long, massive bodies and thick legs. Even kittens are substantially proportioned.

The Birman's long coat creates a look of overall elegance.

There should be a strong ruff, meaning a collar of hair, around the neck.

COLOUR PATTERN

Two elements go into creating the Birman coat pattern. Basically the pattern is that of the Siamese. This means the mask, ears, legs and tail are clearly defined with dense pigmentation as compared to the much paler body colour. This effect is not so apparent in kittens, but develops progressively with maturity. The mask is connected to the ears by tracings.

The Birman pattern is thermosensitive, which means it becomes slightly darker in cold weather and lighter in warm climates. It is due to this fact that kittens are born without colour points. These develop as the body extremities cool down during the days after the kitten is born. For this same reason, the pointed colours get darker as the cat ages due to the blood circulation's becoming less efficient at the bodily extremities.

The actual mutation that creates the Birman pattern is known as the Siamese colour restriction. This degrades black to a very dark brown while also restricting the amount of colour pigment on the cat's body.

The second element of the Birman pattern is the white feet, which are an important breed characteristic. It should be stated that the ideal feet markings are rarely achieved, its being a case of how close these come to the ideal. This is because the white-spotting gene mutation, which creates the white, is very variable—thus unpredictable—in its expression.

Front Paws: These are called gloves and should be pure white. They should be symmetrical and create a straight line across the paw at the point where the angle of the paw changes to that of the leg.

Rear Paws: These gloves are alternatively called gauntlets. They should be pure white and cover the entire paw, tapering up the back of the leg in an inverted 'V' pattern to a point just below the hock. The tapering part of the white is called the lace. The colour of the paw pads in this breed is not important.

Breed Faults: Coloured hairs in the white gloves, lack of white on the paws, unsymmetrical white

BIRMAN COLOURS

SEAL POINT
A dark seal brown. Body is pale beige, also described as a warm fawn to cream. There should be a golden cast, also called a halo, to the back and sides. Nose leather matches points colour.

BLUE POINT
This is a blue-grey contrasting against the cold-toned bluish-white body. Nose leather matches points colour. This colour is created by a mutation that dilutes black pigment. It appears blue-grey due to the dark pigment being spread more thinly within cells of each hair shaft.

CHOCOLATE POINT
A warm milk chocolate. The body is ivory while the paw pads match the points. Heavy rings of pigment on the tail of a mature cat are faults. This colour is the result of a mutation that reduces black pigment to brown.

LILAC POINT
A pinkish-grey, also described as a frost-gray in America. Body is an off-white magnolia. Nose leather pinkish, faded lilac or lavender pink. The colour is the dilution of chocolate created by introducing the dilution gene via crossing to the blue Birman.

RED POINT
An orange-red contrasting with a pale cream that shows a faint golden hue or halo. Nose leather is pink. The introduction of the red gene to the Birman was a bone of contention and remains so to this day, especially in America. Traditionalists feel that the Birman was originally, and should remain, a breed restricted at the most to the four classic Siamese colours.

CREAM POINT
A cream contrasting against an off-white body colour that should display a faint golden hue. Nose leather pink. This colour is the dilution of red and is therefore sex-linked.

In either the red or the cream, faint tabby markings and tail-rings, especially in kittens, are not held to be major faults. The same is true if freckles are seen on the eyelids, nose, ears or lips.

gloves and any white hairs, spots
or blotches on the body, chest,
face or ears. Non-blue eye colour.
Any tendency towards either
Siamese or Persian head structure.

COLOURS

Presently there are 20 varieties of
the Birman. These cover six
colours and three pattern types—
tabby point (in six colours), tortie
point (in four colours) and the
tortie tabby point (in four
colours). The original Birman
colour was the seal point, though
blue also has been within the
breed since its early development
years. The chocolate, the lilac and
red series were added later. The
colour refers to that of the bodily
extremities. The body will be a
much paler shade.

Each of the first three extra
colours came as no surprise, as
the Siamese used in the breed's
development carried them in
recessive form. In the Cat Fanciers
Association (CFA) of America,
only the original four colours are
accepted within the Birman breed.

But in Britain, and all other major registries in America and other countries, the full 20 options are accepted.

Tabby Point

The tabby pattern is so well known that a detailed description of it is unnecessary. In effect the tabby pattern is overlaid on the pattern of the Birman. The colour-point (Siamese) gene of the Birman reduces the intensity of the tabby pattern on the body, but less so on the bodily extremities (the points). The forehead should display an 'M' mark, while there should be 'spectacles' of light-coloured fur around the eyes. The ears feature 'thumbprints' on a solid-coloured ground. There are incomplete rings around the front legs. The hind legs have solid markings above the rear glove laces. There are numerous and variably sized rings around the tail, whose tip should be a solid colour. The tabby point is available in seal, blue, chocolate, lilac, red and cream. In each instance the tabby colour is overlaid on an agouti ground colour, which is a paler version of the colour in question. Thus, the seal tabby point has seal markings on a pale brown background.

Tortie Point

In this pattern the coloured points are intermingled with shades of light and dark red hairs. It is not

A CAT OF A DIFFERENT COLOUR

Each breed enthusiast must make up his or her own mind on the matter of new colours. However, the reality will be that new colours will become accepted. The major associations reflect the will of the majority of breeders and exhibitors. This so, they will always bow to the consensus of majority opinion in most matters related to colour patterns.

Generally, this means accepting new colours. The reason is that once these have passed through any association's requirements of acceptance, which can take years, it becomes all but impossible to stop the tide of support, especially if the colour is very appealing.

For the potential traditionalist, things will become more difficult, but not impossible. It becomes a case that they must take a greater than average interest in both genetics and pedigrees. Via pedigrees, the traditionalist can avoid the use in their programme of cats that are, or may be, carrying the genes for any new recessive colours added to the breed.

Additionally, in 21st century, it is likely that the development of associations restricted to traditional colours and body types will steadily be formed. Presently there is no capacity within major associations to cater to the needs of both mainstream thinking and the traditional breeder.

Possibly in the future some of the major associations may cater to traditionalists by operating separate registers for these. This would meet the needs of those who feel restrictions should be applied within a breed in respect of colour (and also conformation) and those who do not.

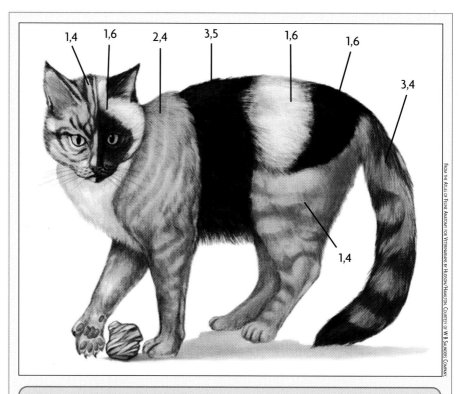

1,4   1,6   2,4   3,5   1,6   1,6   3,4   1,4

From the Atlas of Feline Anatomy for Veterinarians by Hudson/Hamilton. Courtesy of W B Saunders Company.

PARTICOLOURED CAT

Not a new breed of feline, this 'particoloured cat' illustrates the many possibilities of the feline coat. Since cats come in three basic hair lengths, short, long and rex (curly), all three coat lengths are illustrated here. Additionally, different coat patterns, such as mackerel tabby, Abyssinian and self-coloured are depicted to demonstrate the differences.

1–3 COAT TYPES
  1 Shorthair coat
  2 Rex (curly) coat
  3 Longhair coat

4–6 COAT COLOUR PATTERNS
  4 Mackerel (tabby)
  5 Abyssinian
  6 Self-coloured

SKIN AND HAIRCOAT OF CATS

Schematic illustration
of histologic layers of
the integument skin.

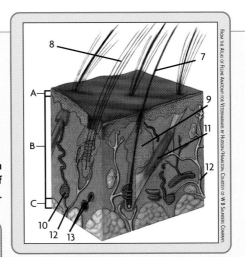

A Epidermis
B Dermis
C Subcutis

7 Primary hair
8 Secondary hairs
9 Area of sebaceous gland
10 Apocrine sweat gland
11 M. arrector pili
12 Nerve fibre
13 Cutaneous vessels
14 Tactile hair
15 Fibrous capsule
16 Venous sinus
17 Sensory nerve fibres
18 External root sheath
19 Hair papilla

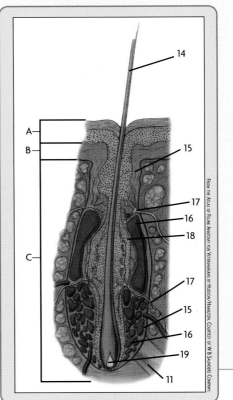

Schematic illustration of
a tactile hair (whisker).

which means, aberrations excepted, it is a female-only pattern. If the dilute gene is present in double dose, these act on the seal to create the blue tortie point, also known as the blue-cream, and on the chocolate to create the lilac point, also called the lilac-cream.

TORTIE TABBY POINTS

This composite brings together both the tabby and the tortie patterns. As with the tortie, the extent and distribution of the light and dark red and cream—depending on the variety—are not important. The two elements of tortie and tabby must be clearly visible. The nose leather will be a mottled pink combined with the appropriate colour of the variety. There are four varieties: seal tortie

necessary that the tortie points be evenly spread on the points, but that each coloured point displays the red colour. The nose leather will match the points colour with or without the addition of pink areas. This pattern is sex-linked,

THE COLOUR RED

In cats, red is what is known as a sex-linked colour. This means it is carried on the X chromosome. An important consequence of this is that if a red male is mated to a non-red female the resulting litter will comprise non-red males and tortoiseshell females. The sex of the breeding pair must be considered when matings involving the red gene are contemplated. The colour of the offspring will be related to their sex. In all other colours, the sex of the mated individuals has no bearing on the colour of their offspring.

tabby point, blue tortie tabby point (blue-cream), chocolate tortie tabby point and lilac tortie tabby point (lilac-cream).

FUTURE BIRMAN COLOURS

In Europe and Australia/New Zealand, breeders have already established the silver, the silver tabby and smoke colour patterns in the Birman breed. These have not as yet gained official recognition, but this can only be a matter of time. Other colours will follow. The Birman of the future will be seen in a very extensive range of colour pattern options. This prediction is based on what has already happened in many breeds, including the Birman (acceptance

As long as there are cats, there will always be new colours to delight—or enrage—the fancy.

of the red series).

Whether or not the addition of more colour patterns are in the best interests of the breed's long-term future, or are even justifiable, is debatable. Potential breeders and exhibitors just entering the breed may have a future interest

A traditional blue point Birman.

The various colours and
patterns create an
array of striking looks
in the Birman.

The various colours and patterns create an array of striking looks in the Birman.

in this subject, so it is worthy of brief discussion.

The questions cannot be viewed in a right or wrong perspective. The Birman, or indeed any other domestic breed, is not a natural animal. It is manmade and was developed from either a hybrid or mutational situation. No specific parameters were ever placed on the Birman, other than in respect of its basic colour pattern and hair length. The breed's conformation is important but is mutable. Colour pattern and hair length are not, at least in the Birman breed. Discussion can therefore only revolve around philosophical viewpoints and potential effects. Traditionalists take the view that the only colours that should be acceptable in the breed are those that were present in it during its years of development. This actually means the seal and the blue. However, most traditionalists

widen this to include the chocolate and the lilac.

Once that development was complete, then no further colours or patterns were justified as they represented unnecessary hybridisation. This detracts from the uniqueness and long-held conception of what a Birman is all about. Additionally, with every new colour pattern that involves recessive genes, the breeder is confronted with a growing number of genetic dilemmas. This is especially so if they wish to specialise in the traditional colours.

The advocates of new colours argue that the introduction of these to a breed does not change its essential characteristics. They believe that new colour patterns are an integral part of a breed's continual development. They also broaden its appeal to potential new owners. Their philosophy is therefore that the Birman should not be static and restricted by old conventions.

Purchasing a

BIRMAN CAT

Given its glamorous appearance, it is no wonder the Birman is so popular. Before the decision to purchase is made, however, careful consideration should be given to the implications and responsibilities of cat ownership. If more owners would do this, there would be far fewer half-starved pets roaming our streets or living in local animal-rescue centres.

OWNER RESPONSIBILITY

The initial cost of a Birman represents only a fraction of its lifetime's cost. The first question is, 'Can you afford one?' The kitten needs vaccinations to protect it against various diseases. Boosters are then required every year. Cat food is more costly than that for dogs. There is also the cost of cat litter every week. Periodic vet checks and treatment for illness or accident must be allowed for. When holidays are taken, you may need to board the pet at a cattery.

From the outset there will be additional costs apart from that of the kitten. It will need a basket, carrying box, feeding and grooming utensils, scratching post and maybe a collar and a few toys. If you have any doubts at all about being able to supply all these needs, it is best not to obtain a cat.

Other matters also need careful thought. If you are planning to have a family, will your love for the Birman be maintained once a baby arrives? Cats are generally not a problem with family newcomers providing they are not ignored or treated as a threat to the baby. Never purchase a kitten for a

It's hard to resist the sweet face of a Birman kitten, but do not make a hasty purchase! Consider the responsibility that cat ownership entails.

DOCUMENTATION

When you take delivery of your kitten, certain paperwork should come with it:

1. 3-to-5 generation pedigree.
2. Breeder-signed registration application form or change of owner registration form. This assumes the breeder has registered stock. If they have not, the kitten cannot be registered at a later date. It is worth less than the kitten with registration paperwork. You are not recommended to purchase a kitten from unregistered parents.
3. Certificates of health, vaccination and neutering, if this has been effected. Ideally, it is desirable that the kitten's parents have been tested negative for major diseases. Additionally, the breeder should know the blood group of your kitten. This may be of importance at a later date.
4. Details of worming or other treatments attended.
5. Diet sheet, feeding timetable and brand names of food items used. This diet should be maintained for at least ten days while the kitten adjusts to the trauma of moving home.
6. Signed receipt for monies paid.
7. Signed copy of any guarantees. Not all breeders give a guarantee on the reasonable grounds that once the kitten leaves their care, its onward well-being is no longer under their control.

Quality breeding will be evident in healthy, attractive and tempermentally sound kittens.

child unless you want one yourself. If you are elderly, it is only fair to consider what would happen to your cherished pet if it were to outlive you or if you were to become hospitalised for long periods.

It is most unfortunate that many people rush into the purchase of cats on impulse. They then find they cannot cope if problems, and extra costs, ensue. Some lose interest in the pet once it matures past its kitten stage. The evidence of these realities is easily seen in the growing number of cats abandoned or taken to animal shelters every year. Invariably, their owners will make feeble excuses for why the cat cannot be kept. In truth, they did not stop to consider at the outset what responsible ownership entailed.

Being such a large hefty cat dictates that the Birman is never going to win a feline gold medal

in athletics. This very fact, however, makes it ideal for certain types of owner. Not every cat lover wants a curtain-climbing, shelf-jumping express train roaring through the house. There are those who believe that being sedate, serene and well mannered are very important traits within any feline that will share their home for maybe 20 or more years.

One of the very nice things about owning a Birman is that you not only get a cat of great beauty, but one that has a truly wonderful nature. The Persian, for at least 50 years before it was used in the development of the Birman, had been bred for impeccable manners. This gave the Birman a good start. From that point onward, breeders maintained and improved on an already sound temperament. The Birman seems to attract breeders who want a cat with a super nature. They endeavour to use only cats with outstanding temperament in their breeding programmes. The present-day Birman is testimony to the success of such a policy.

This is a very gentle breed whose behaviour patterns reflect to a high degree its Persian ancestry. It will be more active than a Persian, meaning playful and adventurous. This is especially so during its youthful years when it will no doubt get

THE PURCHASING PROCESS

Never rush into the purchase of a companion that is to be given the freedom of your home and will become an integral part of your life. A cat may live 20 or more years. This is a long time. It is very prudent to take all those steps that will minimise the chances of your ever regretting the choice you make. Once you have decided on the sex, age, reason for purchase (pet, show or breeding) and desired colour pattern, proceed cautiously, heeding all the advice given here. By following a planned process of selection, you will also gain much useful information.

into plenty of mischief without ever maturing to become a real hooligan. Its conformation allows for a reasonable level of activity until its mature weight and changing inclinations slow it down somewhat.

The Birman is quite intelligent without being a feline Einstein. This reflects the fact

that Siamese genes are in its ancestry. The breed cannot be regarded as an example of the intrepid feline hunter. It has long ago lost the desire and skills needed to outwit its potential prey. Of course, the Birman isn't aware of its shortcomings in this direction. It therefore still goes through the motions of stalking, despite the fact that it just isn't very good at it.

However, this loss of killer instinct no doubt accounts to a high degree for its wonderfully gentle disposition. It loves to be with its owner at all times and can be quite vocal when wanting attention. Its voice is soft and chirp-like. It will settle into most households, including those with other pets, without undue problems. However, it is probably seen at its best in a cat-only home. Ideally it will have a companion of its own breed or one with a comparable nature so that it does not get bullied. Its owner too should have a temperament that complements the breed. This translates to a generally quiet and considerate person, able to appreciate the serene beauty of body and mind that is so typical of the Birman.

Aggression is as alien to a Birman as it can be in any cat. For this breed to be anything other than sweet-natured would mean its home life left a great deal to be desired. Even a poorly

TAKING KITTY HOME

Arrange collection of the kitten as early in the day as possible. If a long journey is involved, be sure to take a few breaks so kitty does not suffer from travel sickness. Do not make stops to show the kitten to friends; this represents a health hazard. Once home, offer the kitten a drink, then allow it to sleep if it so requires. Children must be educated to handle a kitten gently, never to tease it and to respect its sleeping privacy. Until it is litter-trained it should be restricted to the kitchen or another room with an easy-to-clean floor surface.

Pet shops sell a wide array of scratching posts that are of the highest quality.

HOMEMADE TOYS

Cats love to play and pet shops have many cat toys to choose from. Sometimes, however, people give their cats homemade toys. These can be harmful to your cat, as they could have pieces that could break off and be swallowed. Only give your pet toys from the pet shop that have been proven safe for cats.

such as the elderly, may benefit by avoiding the demanding needs of a young kitten. In both these instances, a good age is when the youngster is 9–15 months old. Even a fully mature Birman may prove an excellent choice for some owners.

Kittens should not be obtained under 12 weeks old, though 14–16 weeks is better. No reputable breeder will sell them younger than this. Less caring breeders will let them go to new homes as young as eight weeks of age. Such juveniles will barely have been weaned. They will not have developed the needed resistance to major diseases. They are more likely to become stressed by the premature removal from their mother and siblings. Their vaccinations will not be fully effective. These facts will dramatically increase the risk of immediate problems.

bred Birman would likely still possess an outstanding tempera-ment.

KITTEN OR ADULT?
Most potential owners normally want a kitten because it is so cute, cuddly and playful. A kitten is easily trained and has not yet developed bad habits, which an older Birman may have done. This said, if you plan to breed or exhibit, there are advantages in obtaining a young adult. Other potential owners,

SEX & COLOUR PATTERN
If it is to be purely a pet, the Birman's gender is unimportant. Both are delightful. Males are usually larger, bolder and more outgoing. Females tend to be more discerning about which humans they like. However, each Birman is an individual. Its character and health, more than its sex, should be the basis of selection. Again, the sex is unimportant for the potential exhibitor. It is not even necessary

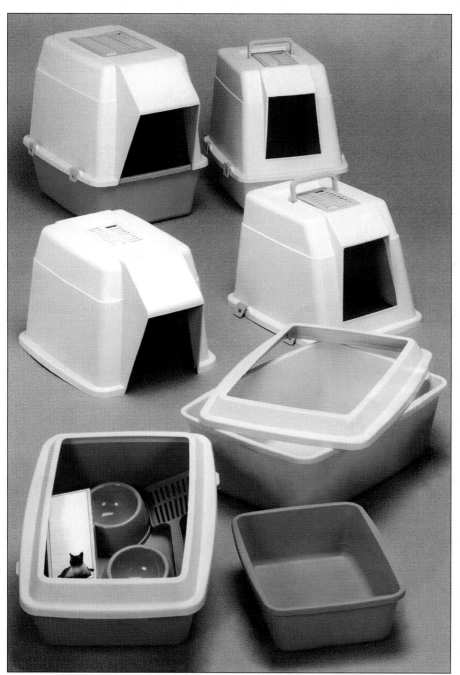

Your local pet shop sells covered and open litter boxes that are suitable for your Birman.

for the cat to be sexually 'entire.' Classes for neuters are featured in shows.

Those with breeding aspirations are advised to obtain only females. All pet owners should regard neutering (males) and spaying (females) as obligatory. Today this can be effected at any age after eight weeks.

The colour pattern is a matter of personal preference. It should never be placed ahead of health and character. Some colours and patterns will be more readily available than others will. The more popular varieties may be less costly than the rarer ones. This would generally not apply to prospective breeding or exhibition individuals where type quality will be as important as colour or pattern.

The playful Birman kitten needs stimulation to keep its mind and body active.

LOOK BEFORE YOU LEAP

It is important that you view as many Birman kittens as you can. This gives you a good mental picture of what a healthy typical example should look like and cost for the quality and colour you want. Normally, you will get what you pay for. If you look for the cheapest kitten, there will be a sound reason why it is the cheapest!

The best place to start your search is at a cat show. At these, most of the colour varieties will be on display. Purchase the show catalogue. It lists all the exhibitors and their addresses. You can see if any live in your immediate locality. Whenever possible, it is best to purchase locally so you can visit the home of the breeder. Some will insist you do so in order to be satisfied that you will make a good owner.

Shows and breeders are advertised in the various cat magazines. You can also contact a major cat registry. They will supply a list of national and regional clubs, which are usually able to supply breeder lists. When visiting a breeder, always make an appointment. Try to visit no more than one a day. This reduces the risk you may transport pathogens (disease-causing organisms) from one establishment to the next. Selecting a good breeder is a

Kittens should be the picture of good health and alertness, with shiny coats and bright, clear eyes.

case of noting the environment in which the cats are kept, the attitude of the owner to you and his cats, and how friendly and healthy the kittens look. It is vital the chosen kitty has an outgoing personality. It must not appear timid or very shy. This indicates a lack of breeder socialisation or a genetic weakness in its temperament. Either way, it is not a kitten you should select.

CHOOSING A KITTEN

If you choose the breeder wisely, and especially if a friend recommends him, this will remove potential problems related to your making a poor choice. However, a little knowledge on what to look for will not go amiss. Observe the kittens from a distance to ensure none is unduly lethargic, which is never a good sign. If any display signs of illness, this should bring to an end any further thoughts of purchase from that source. A reputable breeder would not allow an ill kitten to remain within its litter.

It is always advisable to select a kitten that shows particular interest in you. Birmans are very discerning. If both of you are drawn to each other, this will greatly enhance the bonding essential for a strong relationship.

Once a particular kitten has been selected, it should be given a close physical inspection. The eyes and nose must show no signs of weeping or discharge. The ears will be erect and fresh-smelling. The coat should look healthy, never dry and dull. There must be no signs of parasites in the fur. There will be no bald areas of fur, nor bodily swellings or abrasions. Lift the tail and inspect the anal region. This must be clean, with no indication of congealed faecal matter. Any staining of the fur indicates current or recent diarrhoea.

The kitten must not display a potbelly, which may indicate worms or other internal disorders. Check the teeth to be sure of a correct bite. Bear in mind that the jawbones do not

A HEALTHY KITTEN

Closely inspect any kitten before making a final decision. Keep in mind the following points:

Eyes and nose: Clean and clear with no signs of discharge.

Ears: Fresh-smelling and erect.

Coat: Healthy, not dull or dry.

Anal region: Clean with no staining of the fur.

Feet: Four toes on each foot, plus a dewclaw on the inside of each front leg.

Teeth: Correct bite.

There should be no signs of parasites or bald areas of fur. A potbelly may indicate worms.

ADOPTING AN ADULT

Some owners, such as the elderly, may benefit by adopting an adult cat. They can avoid the demanding needs of a young kitten and enjoy the advantages of a well-trained adult, making grooming an easier task. Breeders and exhibitors can also benefit from purchasing an older cat because it is easier to assess the quality. Sometimes, though, older cats can have bad habits that are hard to break. So if you are thinking about obtaining an older cat, it is important to thoroughly investigate possible behavioural and health problems.

develop at the same rate. Minor imperfections may correct themselves (they may also get worse), but major faults will not. Inspect the feet to see that there are five toes on the front feet, including a dewclaw on the

Your local pet shop will have a variety of cat toys with which you can entertain yourself and your cat.

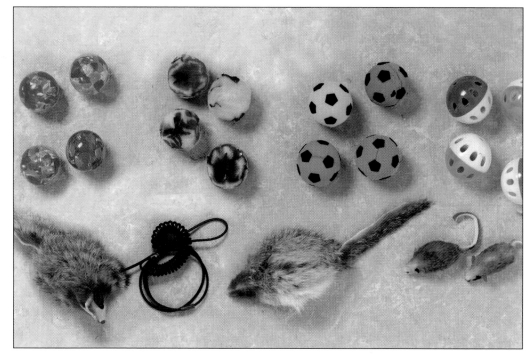

Lightweight collars and leads are available at your local pet shop.

CAT LITTER

The litter that is used in cat boxes can be very variable and in many cases cats reject the use of a cat box because of the litter. Certainly if your cat rejects the use of the cat box, you should try different litters. You can start with the litters available at your local pet shop, then you can try sand, dirt, old rags, cedar shavings or whatever will appeal to your cat. Several cat owners grow clover in a tray and their cats seem to prefer that. However, the tray is kept outdoors and the cats may simply be marking the clover tray rather than using it for elimination purposes.

inside of each front leg, and four on the rear feet.

With respect to the colour, there is no link between this and health other than deafness in certain white varieties. Any faults in the colour or its placement will only be of importance in breeding or exhibition individuals. The potential breeder/exhibitor should obtain a copy of the official standard so they are *au fait* with all colour, pattern and bodily faults of the breed.

KITTY SHOPPING SPREE

Certain accessories should be regarded as obligatory and obtained before the kitten arrives at your home.

SCRATCHING POST

This will save the furniture from being abused! There are many models, some being simple posts, while others are combined with play stations and sleeping quarters. These are the best.

LITTER TRAYS

Some are open trays; others are domed to provide extra privacy. Yet others have special bases in which odour removers are fitted.

A carrying box is an absolute necessity for transporting your pet to the vet. It is also needed if you intend to travel with your Birman.

Litter-box liners are available to make cleaning your cat's litter box an easy task.

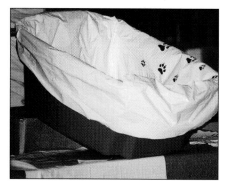

CAT LITTER
There are numerous types on the market, each offering advantages and drawbacks. Avoid the low-cost types that contain a lot of dangerous dust. Use those that are fully biodegradable.

FOOD/WATER DISHES
Polished metal has the longest wear life. Earthenware is less costly than metal and superior to the plastic types.

GROOMING TOOLS
These will comprise a good-quality bristle brush, a fine-toothed comb, nail trimmers, and a soft chamois leather.

CAT COLLAR AND/OR HARNESS
Select elasticised collars. Be sure a name and address disc or barrel is fitted to this. A harness must be a snug but comfortable fit if it is to be effective.

CARRYING BOX
This is essential for transporting the cat to the vet or other places, as well as for home restriction when needed. Be sure it is large enough to accommodate a fully-grown Birman, not just a kitten. The choice is between collapsible models, soft plastic types and, the best choice, those made of wood or fibreglass.

While lead-training a dog is common, cats rarely submit to walking on a leash.

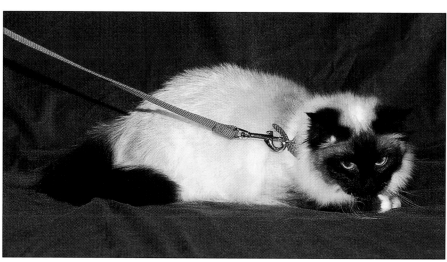

For a kitten, its human environment holds many dangers. Its owner must protect it from these until it becomes agile and wiser. The following dangers lurk in typical households. Always check whether there are additional ones in your home. The most important decision you need to make from the outset is whether or not the kitten is to be given outdoor liberty.

HOW MUCH FREEDOM?

More than at any time in the past the question of how much freedom a cat should be given is the subject of heated debate. It is a very subjective matter. Here the more pertinent points are given so you can relate these to your home location. This, to a very large degree, should influence your decision.

Cats living in or close to an urban area are at the highest safety risk. The amount of traffic is such that death from road accidents is a major concern. In such environments there are high dog populations, some of which are feral. Injury or death from dog attacks is therefore another major source of danger to a feline.

Urban cat populations are also extremely high. Far too many cats are living a virtually feral

BE ONE JUMP AHEAD

Seemingly innocuous things, such as doors, can become life-threatening should they suddenly slam shut on a kitten due to a through draught. When windows and external doors are open, be sure internal doors are secured with a doorstop. At all times be one jump ahead of a kitten in terms of identifying dangerous situations.

THE GARAGE AND SHED

These two buildings are very dangerous to a kitten. Sharp and heavy tools, nails, glass jars, garden weed killers and open tins of paint are but a sampling of the items the average family uses or stores in these. A kitten may clamber into the engine compartment of a vehicle. This could be fatal if the owner happened to start the engine before the kitten had removed itself. Always know where the kitten is.

existence. These are tough, street-wise cats that often carry fleas and other parasites that are vectors of disease. Some will be carriers of, or infected with, feline leukaemia

The warmth of a spin dryer appeals to most cats, so Birman owners must always check the dryer before closing the door.

and other deadly diseases.

The typical feline family pet can be badly injured if it becomes engaged in fights with these roaming bullies. Furthermore, their very presence in and around a gentle cat's garden can cause the pet severe stress. This can make it fearful of stepping outside its home. In some instances, it may cause the pet to actually leave its home.

Sadly, if these risks are not enough, there is no shortage of people who will steal a pedigreed cat, the more so if it is friendly. Add to this the number of abusive people who do not like cats roaming into their gardens, and the scenario is not good. Finally, free-roaming cats also take a heavy toll on local bird and wildlife populations.

Taking these various facts into account, the urban cat is best kept indoors. It can enjoy the benefit of the outdoors if supplied with a roomy aviary-type exercise pen. Some cats can be trained to walk on a lead. This allows outdoor enjoyment, even if this is restricted to the garden. When walking your cat in public places, use only a harness. This is much safer than a collar.

In contrast to urban situations, the cat living in a rural environ-ment is far safer, the more so if there are no immediate neighbours or busy roads. Even so, it is wise to restrict the cat's outdoor freedom to daylight hours. During the night it is more likely to get run over or to threaten local wildlife.

Those living between the extremes of isolated areas and busy urban environments should consider the local risk factor. Generally, it is best to keep the cat indoors but to provide an outdoor exercise pen.

The kitchen poses many dangers to your Birman. Keep the curious cat away from stovetops and other dangerous surfaces.

HOUSEHOLD DANGERS

Within its home, a kitten is best viewed as an accident waiting to happen! The most dangerous room is the kitchen. Hot electric hobs, naked flames from gas rings, boiling pans of food or water and sinks full of water are obvious hazards. An iron left on its board with cable trailing to the floor is an invitation to a kitten to jump up—with potentially fatal

Keep toilets closed to avoid your Birman swimming in or drinking from the bowl!

consequences. Washing machines or spin dryers with warm clothes in them, and their doors open, are inviting places to nap. Always check that the kitty isn't inside if the door has been left open. Cupboards containing poisonous or other dangerous substances should always be kept securely closed.

In the living room the normal dangers are aquariums without hoods, unguarded fires, electric bar heaters, poisonous indoor plants, trailing electrical wires and ornaments that may be knocked over by a mischievous kitty. Toilets can be fatal to an over-curious kitten. The same is

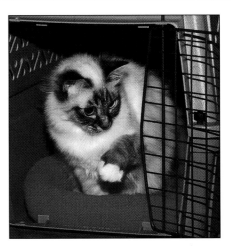

true of a bath containing water. Balconies should be safeguarded to remove the potential for the kitten to slip and fall.

THE TRAVELLING CAT

Whenever your cat needs to be taken on a car journey, never let it travel loose in the vehicle, which is illegal. It must always be in its carrying box. If a cat were to go under the clutch or brake pedal when the car was moving, this would be dangerous to all occupants. A cat might also spring from one seat to another, which might distract the driver. This could have disastrous results.

Never leave a cat alone in a car on a hot day. The temperature can rise dramatically to the point that the cat is unable to breathe. It could die of heat stroke. Always leave a window partially open, but not so much that the agile cat could escape.

OTHER DANGERS

Other potential dangers are when electric tools are left lying about and connected to power outlets— even worse if they are left on, as with bench saws. If the kitten is given freedom to exercise in a garden containing a pond, the kitten must be under constant supervision. Cherished ornaments should be placed out of reach of the kitten, as much for their safety as for any danger they may present to the kitty. It's not always the direct danger of something that can be the problem. If an ornament or similar item crashes to the floor, this can startle the kitten into a panicked departure! The kitten could then fall from a shelf in its haste.

Feeding Your

BIRMAN CAT

Today the feeding of cats has been reduced to its most simple level with the availability of many scientifically prepared commercial diets. However, this fact can result in owners becoming casual in their approach to the subject. While the main object of a given diet is to provide the ingredients that promote healthy growth and maximum immunity to disease, it also fulfils an important secondary role.

A proper diet must maintain in the cat a psychological feeling of well-being that avoids nutritionally related stress problems or syndromes. By ensuring the diet is balanced, of good variety and never monotonous, these dual roles will be achieved. This approach will also avoid the situation of the cat's becoming a finicky eater.

BALANCE AND VARIETY
A balanced diet means one that contains all of the major ingredients—protein, fats, carbohydrates, vitamins and minerals—in the ratios needed to ensure maximum growth and health. Variety means

Offer your kitten the same food that the breeder has used. Initiate dietary changes gradually so as not to upset a young cat's digestive system.

supplying foods in a range of forms that will maintain and stimulate the cat's interest in its meals. Commercially formulated foods come in three levels of moisture: low, semi-moist and moist (tinned foods).

Generally, the dried and moist

Dried foods can be supplied on a free-choice basis. Most Birmans will only eat exactly how much they require to stay fit.

IMPORTANT DON'TS

• Do not let your cat become a fussy eater. Cats are not born fussy but are made that way by their owners. Your cat will not starve if given the correct food, but it may try to convince you otherwise. However, a cat that refuses all foods offered may be ill. Contact your vet.

• Do not give a cat sweet and sticky foods. These provide no benefit and, if eaten, will negatively affect normal appetite for wholesome foods.

• Do not feed vitamin and mineral supplements to either kittens or adults unless under advice from a veterinary surgeon. Excess vitamins and minerals can be as bad for their health as a lack of them. They will create potentially dangerous cellular metabolic imbalances.

• Do not give any questionable foods, such as those that smell or look 'off.' If in doubt, discard them. Always store foods in cool darkened cupboards. Be sure all foods from the freezer and refrigerator are fully thawed.

Purchase the best quality that you can afford when purchasing items for your Birman.

forms are the most popular. Dried cat foods have the advantage that they can be left in the cat dish for longer periods of time than tinned foods. They are ideal for supplying on a free-choice basis. Like the tinned varieties, they come in a wide range of popular flavours.

In order to meet the specific needs of a kitten, there are specially formulated foods available. These contain higher protein levels needed by a growing kitten. As it grows, the kitten can be slowly weaned onto the adult types. There are also special brands available from vets for any kitten or cat that may have a dietary problem as well as special diets for the older cat. These may need lower ratios of

certain ingredients, such as proteins and sodium, so as to reduce the workload of the liver.

Flavours should be rotated so that interest in meals is maintained. This also encourages familiarity with different tastes. Naturally, Birmans will display a greater liking for certain flavours and brands than for others.

FRESH FOODS

To add greater variety and interest, there are many fresh foods that Birmans enjoy. Some will be very helpful in cleaning the teeth and exercising the jaw muscles. All have the benefit of providing different textures and smells that help stimulate the palate. Feed these foods two or three times a week as treats or

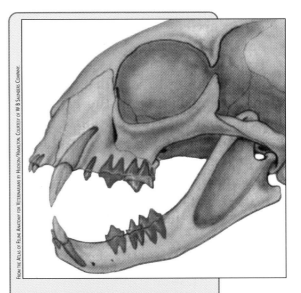

FROM THE ATLAS OF FELINE ANATOMY FOR VETERINARIANS BY HUDSON/HAMILTON. COURTESY OF W B SAUNDERS COMPANY.

MEET THE MEAT-EATERS

Since cats are carnivorous, their teeth are designed to bite and cut. Except for crunching dried foods, cats do very little chewing. They have the fewest teeth of any common domestic mammal— typically 30 (although there are some variations). The canines usually are more developed than the incisors.

DRIED FOOD— MORE WATER

If the cat is only given dried foods, it is essential that its water bowl is always full; it will need to drink more. But it is best to give both dried and moist food types. This minimises the risk of urological problems created by pH alkalinity associated with dried diets.

occasionally as complete meals.

Cooked poultry, including the skin but minus the bones, is usually a favourite, as is quality raw or cooked mincemeat. Cooked beef on the bone gives the cat something to enjoy. Cooked white fish, as well as tinned tuna or sardines, is an example of an ocean delight. Never feed raw

HIGH-QUALITY FOOD

The value of a cat food is determined by its protein/carbohydrate compositions. High-quality foods will contain more protein. The cat is a prime predator and needs a high proportion of protein in its diet.

HOW MUCH TO FEED

Food intake is influenced by many factors. These are the cat's age, activity level, the ambient temperature (more is eaten in the colder months), the cat's breeding state (rearing kittens) and the quality of the food. Always follow the breeder's recommendations on diet until your kitten has settled into your home. Thereafter the needed quantity will increase as the kitten gets older, until full maturity at about two or three years of age.

As a basic guide, a four-month-old kitten will require four meals a day. At six months old, one meal can be dropped. By twelve months of age, only two meals will be required, possibly only one if dried foods are also available on a free-choice basis. As the number of meals is decreased, the quantity must be increased.

fish; this can prove dangerous, even fatal. Although cats rarely enjoy items such as rice, pasta or cooked vegetables, these can nonetheless be finely chopped and mixed with meats or fish. Some Birmans may develop a taste for them. Various cheeses and scrambled or boiled eggs will often be appreciated—but never give raw eggs.

If the diet is balanced and varied, the addition of vitamin and mineral supplements is unnecessary and can actually prove dangerous. While certain of these compounds are released from the body if in excess, others are not. They are stored and can adversely affect efficient metabolism. If a cat shows loss of condition and disinterest in its food, discuss its diet with a vet.

MILK AND CATS

Milk, although associated with cats, is not needed once kittenhood has passed. Indeed, excess can create skeletal and other problems. Some cats may become quite ill if given too much. They are unable to digest its lactose content. However, small amounts may be appreciated as a treat. Goat's milk, diluted condensed milk and low-lactose milks are better than cow's milk.

DIETARY DIFFERENCES BETWEEN CATS AND DOGS

You should never feed your cat dog food because dogs and cats have different dietary needs. Cats have a much higher need for fats than dogs, and kittens need more than adult cats. Cats also require unusually high levels of dietary protein as compared with dogs. The foods you choose for your cat must supply these essential components.

FOOD AND WATER CONTAINERS

Birmans are not too fussy over what vessels are used for supplying their food and water, but a few tips are useful. Birmans do not like to eat from dirty dishes anymore than you would. Their food bowl should be washed after each meal. Water containers should be washed and replenished every day. Saucers make ideal food plates. Wide feeders from your pet shop are excellent for dried biscuits. Pot or polished metal containers are better buys than plastic. They last longer and are easier to keep clean.

WHERE AND WHEN TO FEED

Usually, the best place to feed a cat is in the kitchen. It is important to place food and water dishes as far away from the litter tray as possible. This could otherwise deter the cat from eating. Cats also like to eat in quiet comfort. Meals should be spread across the entire day. When the number is reduced to two, these should be given in the morning and evening at convenient times. For the Birman given outdoor freedom, it is best to feed the main meal in the evening. This encourages it to come home at this time. It can then be kept indoors overnight.

ESTABLISHING DAILY INTAKE

Quoting amounts needed is impossible because of the varying factors mentioned. The best way to establish requirements is on an actual consumption basis. Place a small amount of food on the dish and see how quickly this is eaten. If all is devoured within a few minutes, add a little more. Repeat this until the kitten/cat is satiated and walks away from its dish. Do likewise at the other meals and you will quickly establish daily intake.

Grooming Your
BIRMAN CAT

If your Birman's coat is not cared for on a daily basis, it will soon look bedraggled and cause considerable discomfort to your cat. Mats will form that will prevent dead hair from being shed. These will soon enough become entangled with other debris—grass, small sticks, cat litter and even food. It is, therefore, most important that a prospective Birman owner fully accepts that grooming is crucial with this breed. It should never be a chore. If done regularly, it will help bond the cat to its owner. The cat will always be a joy to behold and its owner will be very proud.

Begin brushing your Birman on the neck and progress down the fur to the tail.

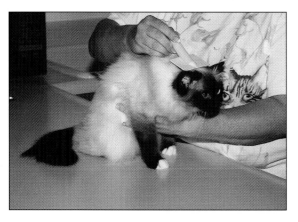

Regular grooming also enables close examination of the cat for any signs of problems. These include fleas or mites, small wounds, abrasions, swellings and bald areas. The grooming process should include inspection of the cat's ears, eyes, teeth and nails.

Always purchase the best-quality items. Avoid the use of low-cost plastic-toothed combs and brushes. These create static electricity. This results in fly-away and crinkled hair that is not the best state for this breed's coat.

Before we discuss grooming procedures, a few general points should be made. If grooming is not to be reduced to a battle between cat and owner, it is essential that the kitten finds this a pleasurable experience. This will not be the case if the owner is heavy-handed in his or her use of the brush, and more especially the comb. The most tender parts of the cat are its underbody parts and tail. These must be groomed with this fact always in mind, doubly so if tags have formed.

Some owners groom the cat on their laps, others on tables. This author prefers a table. Ensure the surface is of a non-slip type—a rubber mat is recommended for this purpose. Again, some owners will commence with the comb, but it is better to use the brush first. It is more forgiving, thus gentle. It avoids unnecessary pulling of the hair.

BRUSHING

Commence on the neck and brush down the fur to the tail. This will remove any small bits of detritus in the coat. Next brush down the chest, body sides and flanks. With the kitten now familiar with the feel of the brush, gently turn and secure the kitty on its back while its belly is brushed. Groom the tail by forming a parting with the brush and grooming the fur at right angles.

This completed, brush against the lie of the fur. Begin on the neck and brush a few inches at a time, working around the body as before. As each small area is commenced, a little baby powder can be sprinkled around the hair roots. As this is brushed and combed out, it will clean the fur, remove grease and help to keep it tag-free. Talcum powder can be used, but it may cause irritation. Powdered chalk is

GROOMING EQUIPMENT

The following will be required for complete grooming:
1. Round-ended, cushioned pin brush
2. Bristle brush
3. Medium-toothed metal comb with handle
4. Flea comb
5. A pair of guillotine nail clippers
6. Baby powder (If the cat is dark coloured and required for exhibition, a soft chamois leather is useful.)
7. Supply of cotton wool and cotton buds
8. Plastic pouring jug
9. Spray attachment for taps
10. Cat shampoo (Those for dogs are not suitable for felines. A baby shampoo can be used but is not as effective as one formulated for cats.)
11. One or two quality towels
12. Good hair dryer (The quieter the better)
13. Non-slip rubber mat
14. Good-sized plastic bowl with a rubber mat placed inside (to use as bath if sink is not suitable.)
15. Medium-soft toothbrush and feline toothpaste (A saline solution is an alternative, but is less tasty.)
16. An appropriately sized plastic or other container in which to keep kitty's boutique apparel

HAIRBALLS (Trichobezoar)

When cats self-groom, they invariably swallow some of their hairs. Normally these do not create a problem. However, if many dead hairs are in the coat, these may be licked and swallowed to accumulate in the stomach as hairballs. These are more common in longhaired breeds than in those with short hair. Hairballs may create intestinal blockages which may so irritate the cat's intestinal tract that it vomits the hairball or voids it via its faecal matter.

If the hairball is not removed, and the cat displays reduced appetite, veterinary assistance is needed. Regular grooming greatly reduces the risk of this condition. Additionally, a teaspoon of liquid paraffin or other laxative once a week may be helpful in cats prone to this problem, but it is unlikely to remove an existing hairball. Pineapple juice containing the enzyme bromelain may break down small furballs. One teaspoonful a day for three days is the recommended dosage.

DECLAWING

Declawing is the surgical removal of all of the claw (or nail) and the first toe joint. This practice is heavily frowned upon and even illegal in some countries, such as the United Kingdom. Unfortunately, in some areas of the world this procedure is still performed. Some owners only have the claws from the front feet removed; others do all four feet. An alternative surgical procedure is removing the tendon that allows the cat to protract its claws. This procedure, referred to as a tendonectomy, as compared to an onychectomy (removal of the claws), is less traumatic for the cat. Claws still must be filed and trimmed after a tendonectomy.

Declawing is not always 100% successful. In two-thirds of the cases, the cats recovered in 72 hours. Only 4–5% of the cats hadn't recovered within a fortnight. About 3% of the cats had their claws grow back!

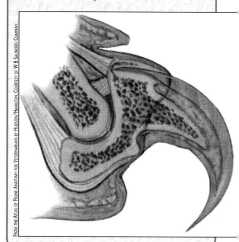

FROM THE ATLAS OF FELINE ANATOMY FOR VETERINARIANS BY HUDSON/HAMILTON. COURTESY OF W B SAUNDERS COMPANY.

A metal comb should be used on the Birman's tail to avoid tangled fur and mats.

another long-established alternative.

Finish by brushing with the lie: the hair should then be tag-free. Now combing will be easier. A tip for show-cat owners is that the use of powder in the coat is most advantageous in the lighter coat colours. Use powder sparingly in the darker ones. The chamois leather is better to polish the darker coat. It produces a better shine than if excess powder has been used.

COMBING

Combing should be done in the same manner as the brushing, except that the final comb need not be done with the lie in most varieties. Combing against the lie is a good opportunity to see if there are any parasites present. These often favour the tail base or the neck behind the ears. If any mats should be found in the coat, these must be teased out using the index finger and thumb of both hands. Be very careful not to pull away from the skin while doing this. It will be painful and the cat will object. Never bath a cat that has even the smallest of mats in its fur. Once soaked, these will shrink into tight balls that will be much harder to tease apart.

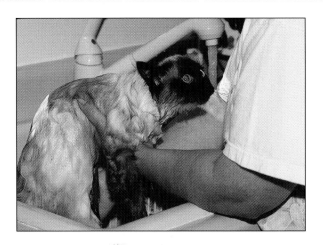

Bathing is rarely enjoyable for a house cat, whether it is a show animal or pet.

Be prepared and efficient to limit the Birman's discomfort. Quick, pleasant baths are the best for the Birman.

Tend to the cat's claws after the bathing is completed.

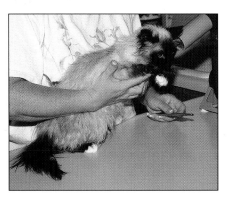

BATHING

During the course of its life, there will usually be a number of occasions when any cat will need a bath, this being more so for a longhaired breed. For the Birman show cat, this will normally be a necessity about seven days prior to a show.

Using the kitchen sink is preferable to a bath. This saves bending and allows for better control of the cat. To prevent the cat from sliding, use a rubber mat. A spray attachment is more efficient than a jug to wet and rinse the coat. The cat should have its own towels.

The choice of shampoo is important. It should ideally be formulated for cats—do not use one for dogs. This could cause problems on a cat's coat. Baby shampoos are the best alternative. Dry shampoos in powder form are available from pet shops. Alternatives would be

CAT COATS

The long primary hairs of longhaired cats can be almost three times as long as those of a shorthaired cat. The genes for length of hair are independent of the genes for colour. The original colour of cats is the mackerel or tiger-striped pattern. This pattern was inherited from the ancestors of the housecat.

talcum powder, powdered chalk or heated bran flakes.

The kitten should be bathed by the time it is six months of

Grooming should always precede bathing, as this will remove any dead hairs. The key to success lies in ensuring that no water or shampoo is allowed to enter and irritate the eyes or ears. You should be able to cope single-handedly with a kitten. However, it may be prudent to have someone else present just in case the adult proves more of a super cat than a kitten!

The water temperature should be warm, never cold or too hot. Prepare a shampoo and

Birmans, like most other cats, are very clean and spend many hours each day grooming themselves. What Birman thinks a human could help a cat groom itself?

age. This will familiarise it with the process before it matures and the process degenerates into a pitched battle. Cats have no love of bathing but can come to accept it if it does not become an unpleasant ordeal.

HAIR GROWTH

Cat's body hairs grow from the follicles, which are connected to the dermis. Tactile hairs (whiskers) are thicker and longer, originating three times deeper than the normal body hairs.

HAIR, HAIR EVERYWHERE!

Cat's hairs grow denser on the abdomen than on the back. The hairs grow according to both light periodicity (daylight versus dark nights) and temperature. Outdoor cats living in colder climates cast their coats twice a year, in the spring and fall, while house cats do so all year long.

water solution before commencing. Have a large towel at hand. Start by soaking the fur of the neck, then work along the back, sides, legs and tail. Pour shampoo onto the back and work this in all directions until the cat has been fully shampooed. Next, thoroughly rinse all the shampoo away. It is essential that none be left in the coat, otherwise it may cause later irritation. The use of a hair conditioner is optional. Its main drawback is that it may make the coats too greasy within days of the bath. Gently but firmly squeeze all water from the coat. The face can be cleaned using a dampened flannel.

Give the cat a brisk rubbing to remove as much liquid as possible from the coat. Now the dryer can be used. Be very careful not to hold this too close to the fur, otherwise it may burn the skin. Keep the nozzle on the move continually. While drying, it is best to be grooming the coat at the same time. This will need the help of another family member to hold the cat while you dry and groom. If the drying process is done correctly, the cat will actually enjoy this part of its grooming once familiar with it.

CLEAN CATS

Cats are self-groomers. They use their barbed tongues and front paws for grooming. Some cats never groom themselves, while others spend up to a third of their waking hours grooming themselves. Licking stimulates certain skin glands that make their coats waterproof.

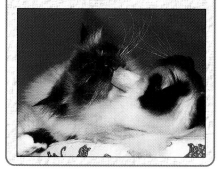

When the cat is dry, it should be given a final good brushing, then kept indoors for a couple of hours to ensure it is thoroughly dry. Baby powder can be used before the final brushing. Your Birman will now look and smell magnificent.

EARS, EYES AND NAILS

When inspecting the ears, look for any signs of dirt. This can be gently wiped away using a dampened cotton bud or one with just a little baby or vegetable oil on it. Never attempt to probe into the ear. If the ear is very waxed, this may indicate any of various health problems. A visit to the vet is recommended. The corners of the eyes can be gently wiped with damp cotton wool to remove any dust that occasionally accumulates.

Inspection of a cat's claws is achieved by firstly restraining the cat while on its back on your lap or held against your chest.

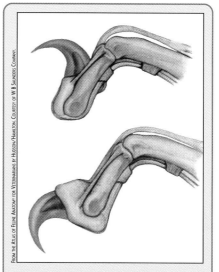

FROM THE ATLAS OF FELINE ANATOMY FOR VETERINARIANS BY HUDSON/HAMILTON. COURTESY OF W B SAUNDERS COMPANY.

RETRACTABLE CLAWS

When at rest, a cat's claws are retracted. The muscles hold the claws in their sheaths. The claw is then extended if the cat wishes to attack prey, defend itself, grab an object or climb. That is why your cat's claws are not always visible. This is true for all species of felines except the cheetah, which is unable to retract its claws, except when it is very young.

PRESS-ON NAILS!

A stylish and fairly successful inhibitor of scratching is a plastic covering on the nails. A plastic sheath is placed over each nail and glued on with a strong, permanent adhesive. Depending upon the cat's activity, these sheaths last from one to three months.

Hold the paw and apply pressure to the top of this with your thumb. The nail will appear from its sheath. If the nail needs trimming, use the appropriate trimmers.

It is vital you do not cut into, or even too close to, the quick, which is a blood vessel. This can be seen as a darker area of the nail in pink-clawed cats. It is more

Never probe in your Birman's ear to clean it. Gently apply a moistened cotton bud to wipe away debris that accumulates there.

difficult, or not possible, to see the quick in dark-coloured nails. In such instances, trim less. You may need a helper to do the trimming or the holding. If in doubt, let your vet do this for you. If cats have ample access to scratching posts, they will only infrequently, if ever, require their nails to be trimmed.

Accustom the kitten to having its teeth wiped and it will more readily accept dental care.

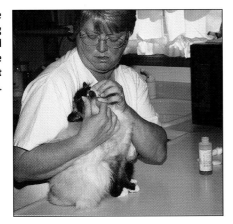

TEETH

From its youngest days, your kitten should become familiar with having its teeth cleaned. Many owners do not give their cats' teeth the attention they

GINGIVITIS
(Plasmocytic-Lymphocytic Stomatitis)

There are many causes of this condition. But the end result is the same—bad breath, excessive plaque, tooth loss and almost certainly pain. The cat salivates excessively, starts to eat less and consequently loses weight. On inspection, the gums are swollen, especially in the area of the premolar and molar teeth. They bleed easily. There are various treatments, such as antibiotics, immunostimulants and disinfectant mouth gel. However, these invariably prove short-term and merely delay the inevitable treatment of extraction.

Prevention avoids this painful condition. Regular tooth inspection and cleaning, plus provision of hard-food items, such as cat biscuits, achieve this to a large extent. There are also special cat chews made of dried fish that help clean the teeth. They also contain antibacterial enzymes that minimise or prevent secondary bacteria from accumulating. Ask for these at your pet shop or vet's surgery. Gingivitis may commence in kittens, so do not think it is something that only occurs in the older cat.

should. This has become progressively more important due to the soft diet regimens of modern cats. Initially, gently rub the kitten's teeth using a soft cloth on which toothpaste has been applied. This will accustom the kitten to having its teeth touched as well as to the taste of the tooth cleaner. When this is no problem for the kitten, you can progress to a soft toothbrush and ultimately one of medium hardness. Periodically let your vet check the cat's mouth.

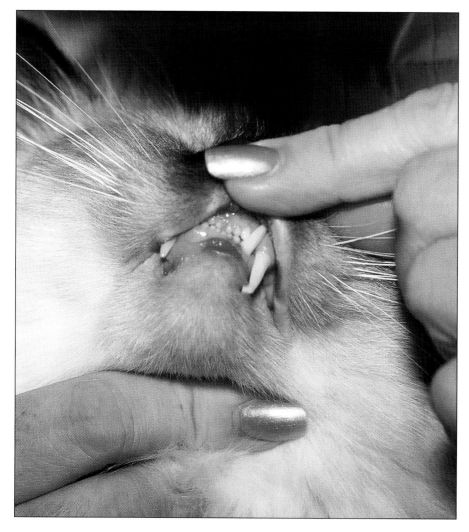

Make tooth care a part of your Birman's grooming and maintenance routine.

Breeding Your

BIRMAN CAT

While the idea of becoming a breeder may appeal to many owners, the reality is more difficult than is often appreciated. It requires dedication, considerable investment of time and money, and the ability to cope with many heart-wrenching decisions and failures.

It would be quite impossible to discuss the complexities of practical breeding in only one chapter, so we will consider the important requirements of being a breeder plus basic feline reproductive information. This will enable you to better determine if, indeed, this aspect of the hobby is for you.

BEING A BREEDER
Apart from great affection for the breed, a successful breeding programme requires quantifiable objectives. Foremost among these is the rearing of healthy kittens free from known diseases. Next is the desire to produce offspring that are as good as, indeed better than, their parents.

Such objectives ensure that a breeder will endeavour to

Socialisation, including playing with siblings, is a vital part of every kitten's development.

TOO MANY CATS

There are already too many cats in the world. In too many countries, thousands of pathetic-looking felines can be seen wandering the streets in a badly emaciated state. They live tormented lives and have become a major social problem in many areas. There can be no excuse for these feral populations in developed Western nations. Quite frankly, some people who own cats, including some pedigree owners, lack a sense of responsibility.

Cats allowed to roam in a non-neutered state are by far the main reason for the overpopulation problem. Unless a cat is of show or breeding quality, there is not a single justification for it to be bred or to remain in a non-neutered state. If your cat was purchased as a pet, you should help to resolve this global problem by having it neutered at the earliest possible date. This will make it a far healthier, better and less problematic pet.

maintain standards and reduce or remove from the breed population any instances of dangerous diseases and conditions. Only stock registered and tested free of major diseases should ever be used. Adopting such a policy helps to counteract those who breed from inferior and often unhealthy cats.

To be a successful breeder, you will need to become involved in the competition side of the hobby. Only via this route will you be able to determine if your programme is successful or not.

Always remember that even the top-winning breeders still produce quite a high percentage of kittens that will only be of pet quality. There will be many disappointments along the road to even modest success.

THE DISADVANTAGES OF BREEDING

There are many rewards to be gained from breeding but the disadvantages should also be carefully considered. Kittens are demanding, especially once they are over three weeks of age.

Rearing, vaccination, registration and veterinary bills will be costly. Any thoughts of profit should be dispelled. Homes must be found for the kittens, which will entail receiving many telephone calls—some at very inconvenient hours.

Many potential buyers will prove to be either unsuitable or 'time-wasters' looking for the cheapest pedigreed cat obtainable. Kittens may die, while cats of any age could test positive for a major disease. They may have to be put to sleep or given to a caring person who understands the problem.

Owning a number of cats will mean investing in cat pens. When females come into heat, they will try to escape and mate with any local tom with a twinkle in his eye! Their scent and calls will attract roving Romeos who will gather near your home and

Accommodating the needs of one pet Birman is much simpler than providing for an entire cattery of breeding animals.

TOM FOOLERY

A non-neutered male cat kept as a single pet has little or no value for breeding purposes. It must be exhibited so it can gain some fame. The owner must have modern facilities to house both males and females. Females are always serviced at the home of the stud owner. This is extra responsibility and cost.

Such a male cannot be given any freedom to roam. If the tom is kept indoors, its scent marking odours will often become intolerable. Even kept outdoors in a suitable cat pen, it will spray regularly to attract the attention of any females in the area. Toms are more assertive and often more aggressive than neutered males.

If they are allowed any outdoor freedom, they will become involved in battles with the local toms. Consequently, they will soon lose their handsome looks! Most cat breeders do not even keep males because of the problems and costs they entail. These cats are best kept in catteries where the owners have the time, the funds, and everything else needed to justify their retention.

involve themselves in a series of raucous battles. Holidays and matings will need to be planned around hoped-for litter dates. All in all, owning only one or two breeding females is a major commitment.

Before deciding whether breeding really is something you want to do, what would make good sense would be to neuter the pet and then become an exhibitor. When you have exhibited a number of times, your knowledge of cats will be greater, as will your contacts. You will be more aware of what quality is all about and what it will cost for a well-bred female. It will be like an apprenticeship. Whether you then become a breeder, remain an exhibitor or prefer life as a pet

CAT CALLS

Females left in a non-spayed state are far more at risk from diseases and infections of the uterus. When in heat, the female becomes unusually affectionate and provocative. Her calls, a sound once heard never forgotten, can become extremely annoying if she is left unmated.

CAVEAT EMPTOR

When purchasing a kitten for breeding, make certain the seller knows what your intentions are. If a kitten is registered on the non-active register, this means it was not considered by its breeder to be good enough for breeding. Any kittens bred from such a cat cannot be registered. You should also check that the mother of the kitten/young adult you are interested in has tested negative for feline leukaemia and that all other vaccinations are current.

Hobby breeders are heartily encouraged to buy a female cat to begin their budding programmes.

owner, you will be glad you heeded the words of advice given here.

STOCK SELECTION

Stock selection revolves around health, quality, sex and age. Before these are discussed, it should be stated that many beginners unwisely rush this process. It is essential that ample time be devoted to researching

THE BREEDING QUEEN

A female used for breeding purposes is called a queen. The principal requirement of such a cat is that she is an excellent example of the breed. This does not mean she must be a show winner. Many a winning exhibition cat has proved to have little breeding value. This is because a show cat gains success purely on its appearance; however, it may not pass those looks to its offspring.

A good breeding female may lack that extra something needed to be a top winner. Yet, she may pass on most of her excellent features to her offspring. Much will depend on the breeding line from which she was produced. Therefore any potential breeder must research existing breeders to ascertain which have good track records of producing consistently high-quality cats. In truth, and sadly, few newcomers in their haste to become breeders make this extra effort. This can result in becoming disillusioned if the female produces only average to inferior kittens.

from whom to purchase. This decision will influence a novice breeder's entire future endeavours.

HEALTH

Cats should only be obtained from a breeder whose stock has been tested negative for FeLV, FIP and FIV. The stock should be current on all vaccinations and worm treatments. Additionally, its blood type should be known so as to avoid incompatibility problems.

QUALITY

This must come in two forms. One is in the individual cat's appearance; the other is in its genetic ability to pass on the quality of its parents. The best way of obtaining these paired needs is to obtain initial stock from a breeder having a proven record of success in Birmans, and with the colour you plan to start

WHAT'S A PEDIGREE WORTH?

When choosing breeding stock, never be dazzled by a pedigree. No matter how illustrious this is, it is only ever as good as the cat that bears it. If the cat is mediocre, then its prestigious pedigree is worthless from a breeding perspective. There are many other pitfalls for the novice when judging the value of a breeding line. These you must research in larger, more specialised books.

with. Being well acquainted with the breed's standard will be advantageous when seeking foundation stock. A female show cat attains her titles based on her appearance, but she may not pass on those looks to her offspring. Another cat that is very sound may pass on most of her good points and thus be more valuable for breeding. Of course, all litters will be influenced by the quality of the tom used. He will account for 50% of the offspring's genes. When viewing a litter of kittens, never forget that they are the result of the genes of two cats.

SEX

The beginner should only obtain females. The best advice is to commence with just one very sound female. By the time you have exhibited her and gained more knowledge about the finer points of the breed, you will be better able to judge what true quality is all about. By then you will also have made many contacts on the show circuit. Alternatively, you may decide breeding is not for you and will have invested the minimum of time and money. A male is not needed until a breeder has become established. Even then, owning one is not essential to success. There is no shortage of quality studs. Males create many problems the novice can do without. Once experience is

THE MALE STUD

The selection of a suitable stud should have been planned months before, as it can take some time to find the best male to use. It is preferred that the breeding lines of the stud are compatible with those of the female, meaning both pedigrees will carry a number of the same individuals in them. This is termed line-breeding. The ideal male will excel in those features that are considered weak in the female. You may read in other books that if a female is weak in a given feature, the ideal stud will be the total opposite. However, this can be misleading.

If the female has an overly long tail, what you do not need is a stud with a short tail. Rather, his tail should be as near the ideal length as possible. Genetically, this will improve tail length in your line without introducing unwanted genetic variance in your stock. Compensatory matings, such as short tail to long tail, will create such variance. Once a male has been selected, ensure all his papers and vaccinations are in order. The female will be taken to the stud and left with him for a few days.

gained is the time to decide if owning a male would be of any particular benefit.

AGE

There is no specific age at which stock should be purchased but the following are suggested.

1. Most people purchase young kittens so they can enjoy them. However, with such youngsters, their ultimate quality is harder to assess.

2. Chances are improved if a

kitten has already won awards in shows. This will be when she is 14 weeks to 9 months of age, but she will be more costly.

3. A quality young female that has already produced offspring is a prudent choice but will be the most expensive option.

THE BREEDING PROCESS

Sexual maturity in cats may come as early as four months of age. Breeding should not be considered until the female is at least 12 months old, especially in the slow-maturing breeds. A young cat barely out of her kitten stage may not have the required physical or psychological stability to produce and raise a vigorous litter. After her first heat, a female will normally come into heat again every two to three weeks and continue to do so until mated. The actual oestrus period lasts 14 days. It is during this time that she is receptive to a male.

Once the mating has been

THE HEAT IS ON

Most female cats reach sexual maturity by the time they are 28 weeks old. Females normally accept males from late winter to early fall, about a six-month period. They have a reproductive cycle of about two weeks and are in heat for about one of the two weeks. Intercourse causes the female to ovulate and pregnancy may last for about 63 or 64 days, perhaps longer in cold climates and shorter in the tropics.

successful, the time between fertilisation and birth of the young, known as the gestation period, is in the range of 59 to 66 days, 63 or 64 days being typical. The litter size will generally be two to five. Kittens are born blind and helpless, but develop rapidly. Their eyes open at about 10 to 14 days. By 21 days they start exploring. At this time they will also be sampling solid foods. By eight weeks they can be vaccinated and neutered if required. Weaning normally commences by the age of six weeks and is completed within two to three weeks. Kittens can go

NEWBORN KITTENS

Most kittens are born with body hair. Their ears and eyes, however, remain closed for about 10 to 14 days, though some ears and eyes become functional after 72 hours. Kittens should be allowed to nurse for seven weeks, longer if they will not readily eat and drink from a plate. If allowed to nurse, most kittens will stay on their mother's milk for two months or more.

ROAMING ROMEOS

Males cats, toms, have extended testicles, very early in life. Within about nine months the tom is capable of mating with a queen. Both queens and toms are polygamous and it is not uncommon for a queen to have a litter containing kittens fathered by different toms.

to a new home when 12 weeks old, though 14 to 16 weeks is preferred. During this period you must decide if you wish to register the kittens or merely 'declare' them. This allows them to be registered at a later time. Obtain the necessary information and forms from your cat-registration authority. You should also consider the benefits of registering your own breeder prefix. This, however, is only worthwhile if you intend to breed on a more than casual basis. If you have decided that certain kittens are unsuitable for showing/breeding, do consider early neutering.

One of the outstanding virtues of cats is that they are easy to live with. They are fastidious in their personal habits related to grooming and toilet routines and basically require very little of their owners. Nonetheless, behavioural problems in cats can occur, and an owner needs to understand all the possible causes and solutions. You may never encounter a single problem with your cat, but it pays to be prepared should your feline charge disrupt your domestic bliss.

THE TRUTH ABOUT CATS AND DOGS

Cats are unique in having the scrotum fully haired, a marked difference from their canine counterparts. This led one keen observer to say that cats were not small dogs! Dogs were domesticated well before cats since cats only served to protect the abode of the owner from rodents, while dogs served as guards, hunters, herders, exterminators and as loyal companions that were readily trainable. Cats have always been more independent and less trainable.

THE BASIS OF TRAINING

The most effective means of training a cat is via reinforcement of success. A cat learning from lavish praise of doing what is required will want to repeat the action to gain more affection. There are no potential negative side effects. Conversely, when scolding or another method of discipline is used, there is always the possibility the cat will not relate the punishment to what the owner had intended.

For example, you cannot discipline for something done in the past. The past is anything much longer than a few minutes ago. If you call the cat to you and punish it for something done hours earlier, it cannot relate to that action. It will relate the discipline to the act of going to you when called! This will create insecurity in the pet, increasing the risk that more problems will develop.

REMEDIAL METHODS

When faced with a problem, firstly try to pinpoint the likely cause(s). Next, consider the remedial options. Be sure these will not result in negative side effects linked to you. Always be the paragon of patience. Some problems may be extremely complex and deeply rooted within the cat's behaviour patterns. As such, they are habits not easily changed and often difficult to analyse. In discussing the following problems, it is hoped you will understand the basic ways to correct other unwanted patterns of behaviour that might occur. But always remember it is far better to avoid a problem than correct it.

THE LITTER TRAY

A very common problem for some owners is that their cat starts to attend to its toiletry needs anywhere other than in its litter tray. The problem may become

WHY WHISKERS?

Cats are famous for their whiskers. The whiskers are tactile hairs by which cats feel. Most tactile hairs are on the cat's face, mostly on the upper lip and around the eyes, and on the wrist (carpus). These carpal hairs are extremely sensitive and are found on many predatory animals that use their front paws for holding their victims.

Play-fighting and posturing are vital components of the feline's behavioural pattern. These two littermates are practising hissing and swatting.

SETTING THE GROUND RULES

From the outset you must determine the ground rules and stick to them. Always remember that your companion's patterns of behaviour begin to form from the moment it first arrives in your home. If the future adult is not to be given outdoor freedom, then do not let it outdoors as a kitten. If any rooms are to be out of bounds to the adult, then do not let the kitten into them. Stability is vital in a cat's life. When this is not so, the result will be stress and its related behavioural changes.

Ground rules of how to handle the kitten and to respect its privacy when sleeping should be instilled into all children. The cat's meals should be given at about the same time each day. This will have the secondary advantage that the pet's toilet habits will be more predictable.

apparent from the time the kitten gets to its new home, or it may develop at any time during its life. So, let us start from the beginning and try and avoid the situation.

Until you are satisfied the kitten is using its litter tray, do not give it access to carpeted rooms. The youngster should already have been litter trained well before you obtained it. You should buy a litter tray similar to the one it is already familiar with. It is also important that the same brand of litter is used, at least initially. Place the tray in a quiet spot so the kitten has privacy when attending to its needs.

A kitten will need to relieve itself shortly after it has eaten, exercised or been sleeping. Watch it carefully at these times. If it stoops to attend to its needs other than in the litter tray, calmly lift it into its tray and scratch at the litter. Never shout or panic the kitty by making a sudden rush for it. If it does what is hoped, give it lots of praise. If it steps out of the tray, gently place it back in for a few seconds.

If nothing happens, be patient and wait, then repeat the process. If it fouls the kitchen floor when you are not watching, simply clean this up and wait for the next opportunity to transport the kitten to its tray. It rarely takes long for a kitten to consistently use this. Be very sure the tray is kept spotless. Cats have no more desire to use a

CAUSES OF LITTER-BOX PROBLEMS

1. The litter tray is dirty. Cats never like to use a previously fouled tray.

2. The litter has been changed to one of a different texture which the cat does not like. Generally the finer-grained litters are the most favoured.

3. A scented litter is being used to mask odours. The cat may not like the scent. Such litters should not be necessary if the tray is regularly cleaned.

4. The tray is regularly cleaned, but an ammonium or pine-based disinfectant is being used. This may aggravate the cat's sensitive nasal mucous membranes. Additionally, the phenols in pine are dangerous to cats.

5. The litter tray is located too close to the cat's food and water bowls. Cats do not like to eat near litter trays or to defecate/urinate close to their feeding areas.

6. Another cat or free-roaming pet has been added to the household and is causing the cat stress. In multi-cat households, two or more trays may be needed.

7. There is insufficient litter in the tray. There should be about 1.5 inches of litter depth.

8. The cat has developed a fear of using the tray due to an upsetting experience. For instance, the owner may have caught the cat as it finished using the tray in order that it could be given a medicine. Children may be disturbing it while it is relieving itself.

9. The cat is ill (or elderly) and is unable to control its bowel movements. Veterinary attention is required.

10. The cat, because of one or more of the previous problems, has established other more favourable areas.

MAN MEETS CAT

Early man, perhaps 8000 years ago, started his symbiotic relationship with domestic cats, *Felis catus* or *Felis domesticus*. The cats killed and ate the rats and mice, and probably anything else which crawled and was small, which early man attracted and considered as pests. Early man reciprocated by allowing the cat to sleep in his cave, hut or tent. Cats, being essentially nocturnal, kept the small mammals (rats, mice, etc.) from disturbing the sleep of early man.

As early man matured to modern man, the domestic cat came along as an aid to pest control. This was especially true of peoples who farmed, as farmers were plagued with rodents. Though most cats were not selectively bred for their predatory skills, it was obvious that those cats that were the best hunters were more successful in evolutionary terms than the cats that were more meek. Modern cats have changed very little from the cats from which they descended. There are still, today, cats that are very predatory, attacking small mammals and birds; there are also meek cats which, unless fed by their owners, would perish in a competitive cat society.

It has been shown repeatedly that if kittens are socialised in a proper manner, they will be peaceful pets. This includes lions and tigers. If the kittens are not socialised properly, they revert immediately to their aggressive, predatory behaviours.

TIDY TOILETING

During the kitten's stay in the nest box, the mother will assist or even stimulate bowel and urine elimination, at least for the first month of the kitten's life. The mother also does the clean up work in the nest box. But once the kitten is older, it becomes capable of relieving itself out of the nest box. Usually the kitten likes sand, soft earth or something that seems absorbent and is easily moved with its paws. By the time the kitten is two months old, it should develop the discipline of covering its elimination. Not all kittens develop this discipline, though the use of an absorbent clay litter seems to be helpful in developing this discipline in young cats. Your local pet shop will have various cat litters to offer you.

fouled toilet than you do. Every few days, give the cat tray a good wash. Use soapy water and always rinse it thoroughly. Allow it to dry, and then fill the tray with litter to depth of about one to two inches.

By identifying the cause(s) of litter-box problems, the correction is often self-evident. However, once the cause has been corrected, this is only part of the solution. Next, the habit of fouling other places must be overcome. Where possible, do not let the cat enter rooms in which it has started to foul until the odour has had time to fully disperse. Wash the area of the fouling. Then treat carpets and soft furnishings with an odour neutraliser (not an air freshener) from your pet shop or vet.

If the cat cannot be prevented from entering certain rooms, then cover previously fouled areas with plastic sheeting or tinfoil, or rinse the area with white vinegar. Also, place a litter tray in the fouled room while the retraining is underway. It may help if a different size, type or colour of tray is used.

SCENT MARKING

Both sexes scent mark, though males are more prolific. It is a means of advertising their presence in a territory, thus an integral part of their natural behaviour. Spraying is usually done against a vertical surface. It tells other males that the individual is residing in that territory. Alternatively, it will tell a female that a male lives close by—or it will tell the male that a female is in the area. It is thus a

CATS AND OTHER PETS

If you already have a pet cat or cats, or dogs, or almost any other animal that isn't small, creeping or crawling, your cat can usually be socialised so the other pet and the cat will tolerate each other. In many cases, cats and dogs become quite friendly and attached to each other, often making frequent physical contacts, sleeping together or even sharing each other's food.

CAUSES OF SCENT MARKING

1. Another cat, or pet, has been introduced to the household. It may be bullying the resident cat. This problem may resolve itself when the two get to know each other. The more cats there are, the longer it may take for the situation to be resolved. Much will depend on the space within which the cats may roam and whether they are able to avoid those they dislike.

2. The birth of a new family member may annoy the cat for a while, especially if its owner suddenly gives it less attention.

3. A friend staying in the home for a few days may not like cats. If 'shooed' away a number of times, the cat may feel it should assert its position and mark it.

4. If the cat is given outdoor freedom, a bully may have moved into the territory. Having lost monopoly of its own garden, the pet may assert its territorial boundaries within its home. If a cat flap is used, another cat may be entering the home and this will trigger the resident to scent mark.

MARKING TERRITORY

Cats are geographical by nature and they mark their territories in the usual way...by spraying their urine. The frequency of spraying is amazing! A non-breeding male cat that is not within its own turf will spray about 13 times an hour while travelling through the new territory. While a breeding male will spray almost twice as much. One reports states that free-ranging males spray 62.6 times an hour–that's more than once a minute!

Cat urine is recognisable for at least 24 hours and male cats spend a lot of time sniffing the area. Females spend less time but both sexes easily recognise the urine from male cats that are strange to the area.

sleeping place if it does not have one may help. Covering the sprayed surface with plastic sheeting, or a cloth impregnated with a scent the cat does not like (such as lemon, pepper or bleach), may be successful. Spraying the cat with a water pistol when catching it in the action is a common ploy. Veterinary treatment with the hormone progesterone may prove effective—discuss this with your vet.

SCRATCHING

Scratching is a normal feline characteristic. Unfortunately, house cats tend to destroy the furniture to satisfy their need to scratch. Feral or outdoor cats usually attack a tree because trees are readily accessible and the bark of the tree suits their needs perfectly. If the outdoor cat lives in a pride, it will scratch more than a solitary feral cat. The reasons for this are known. When cats scratch, they leave telltale marks. Parts of the nail's sheath exudate from glands located between their claws and the visual aspects are the marks that cats leave to impress or advertise their presence.

very important part of a cat's social language.

Neutered cats have little need to mark their territory or leave their 'calling card' to attract mates. They are far less likely to spray than those not altered. However, scent marking may commence when the cat is attempting to assert its position in the household.

To overcome the problem of scent marking, you first need to try and identify if there is an obvious specific cause. In multi-cat households, it also requires positive identification of the sprayer(s) and the favoured spraying surface. Giving the cat more freedom and its own

Cat owners whose cats scratch should not consider the scratching as an aggressive behavioural disorder. It is normal for cats to scratch. Keeping your cat's claws clipped or filed so they are as short as possible without causing bleeding may inhibit scratching. Your vet can teach you how to do this. Clipping and filing should be started when the kitten is very young. Starting this when the cat has matured is much more difficult and may even be dangerous.

There are ways to control annoying cat scratching. Certainly, the easiest way is to present your cat with an acceptable cat scratching post. These are usually available at most local pet shops. The post should be covered with a material that is to your cat's liking. If your cat has already indicated what it likes to scratch, it usually is a good idea to cover the post with this same material. Veterinary surgeons often suggest that you use sandpaper, as this will reduce the cat's nails quickly and it will not have the urge to scratch. Certainly using hemp, carpeting, cotton towelling or bark is worth a try. Once the cat uses the post, it usually will have neither a desire nor a need to scratch anyplace else.

Besides the physical need to scratch, many cats have a psychological need to scratch. This is evidenced by where they scratch versus what they scratch. Often cats prefer semi-darkness. Some prefer flat surfaces and not vertical surfaces. Some prefer public areas in which their human friends are present instead

SCRATCHING FURNITURE

All cats need to scratch in order to maintain their claws in good condition. For this reason, one or more scratching posts strategically placed in the cat's most used rooms will normally prevent the problem. Place the post in front of the scratched furniture. It can be moved steadily further away once the furniture is ignored. This is a problem that may become more manifest when cats are not allowed outdoors and have insufficient indoor provision to scratch.

CAT SCRATCH DISEASE

An objectionable habit of many poorly raised kittens is their exuberant jump to greet you. This flying jump may result in the kitten's being attached to your body; otherwise it will fall to the floor and may injure itself. In the attachment process your skin will usually be pierced and this is a health concern. All cat scratches and bites should be thoroughly cleaned with an antiseptic soap. If a sore appears at the site of the wound, you should visit your family doctor immediately.

Cat scratch disease is a well-known problem. It is caused by a bacterium (*Rochalimaea henselae*) that is usually easily treated with antibiotics. However, more and more cases show resistance to the usual antibiotics.

Untreated catch scratch fever may result in an enlargement of the lymph nodes, imitating a cancerous condition known as lymphoma. Interestingly enough, the lymph nodes, upon biopsy, may show large Reid-Sternberg cells, which are a characteristic of Hodgkins lymphoma. The bottom line is that cat scratches should be taken seriously.

of secluded areas. It may be stress-related, as with scent marking, because scratching is another territorial marking behaviour. In any case, the idea is to get your cat to scratch the post and not the carpets, furniture, drapes or the duvet on your bed.

Introduce your cat to the post by rubbing its paws on the post, hoping it will take the hint. Oftentimes the cat voluntarily attacks the post. Unfortunately, oftentimes it doesn't. If you catch your cat scratching in a forbidden area, startle it with a loud shout, by banging a folded newspaper against your hand or with something else which will take its attention away from scratching. Never hit the cat. This will only get a revengeful reaction that might be dangerous.

RUBBISH RUMMAGING

Cats are inquisitive and may decide to have a good look through any interesting rubbish bins that are exuding an enticing odour. Normally, the answer is to remove the bin. However, if the attraction always seems to be kitchen rubbish, there may be a nutritional problem. Your cat may be searching for food because it is being underfed! It may alternatively be receiving an unbalanced diet and is trying to satisfy its inner need for a given missing ingredient.

Another possibility, and one

which may be more appropriate to the indoors-only cat, is boredom or loneliness. These conditions can only be remedied by greater interaction between owner and cat and/or obtaining a companion feline.

Clearly the cause should be identified. The immediate solution is to place the rubbish in a cupboard or similar place that is out of the cat's reach. This type of solution is called removal of the re-enforcer. It is a common method of overcoming problems across a number of unwanted

THE PICA SYNDROME

The term 'pica' is a veterinary term that refers to a morbid desire to ingest things that are abnormal to the cat's diet. Cats are usually addicted to soft materials like wool, silk, cotton or a mixture of these and synthetic cloths. Hard plastics, wood and even metals have been involved in this pica syndrome. If you observe your cat chewing these fabrics or materials, speak to your vet. Most veterinarians who observe the pica syndrome think it is a nervous problem that can successfully be treated with drugs normally used for depression. In any case, the genetic makeup of your cat should be investigated and if pica occurs with any of the parents or previous offspring, do not breed your cat.

FERAL CATS

Feral cats are, as a general rule, undernourished. They spend most of their time searching for food. Consequently, those feral cats that have kittens spend less time with their kittens than well-nourished cats. It has been shown that kittens born to feral mothers are usually unsocial and show little affection for their mothers. Obviously, they would show a similar lack of affection for a human. That's one of the reasons that feral kittens make poor pets and should neither be adopted nor brought into your home. Kittens, which for any reason are separated from their mothers at the age of two weeks, develop an attitude of fear and wariness. They escape from contact with other cats or humans, and can even be dangerous if they feel trapped.

behaviours. However, it does not correct the underlying problem that must still be addressed.

The first-time cat owner should not think that the problems discussed will likely be encountered. They are only met when the cat's environment is lacking in some way. Always remember that the older cat may have problems with bowel control. An extra litter tray at another location in the home will usually remedy this situation. Finally, if a problem is found and you are not able to remedy it, do seek the advice of your vet or breeder.

CLASSES AT SHOWS

Open	Any cat of the specified breed.
Novice	Cats that have never won a first prize.
Limit	Cats that have not won more than first prizes.
Junior	Cats over nine months of age but less than two years on the day of the show.
Senior	Cats over two years old.
Visitors	Cats living a given distance away from the show venue.
Assessment	Experimental breeds, but which have an approved standard.
Aristocrat	Cats with one or two Challenge Certificates (or Premiers for neuters) so are not yet full Champions/Premiers.

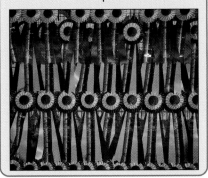

Without shows, the cat fancy could not exist. There would be only a handful of breeds as compared with today's ever-growing list. There would be fewer colour patterns and far less cat awareness. Given the great importance of shows to the cat fancy, it is perhaps a little surprising, and disappointing, that the majority of cat owners have never visited a feline exhibition.

Shows such as the National and the Supreme of Britain, or their equivalents in other countries, are the shop windows of the world of domestic cats. They are a meeting place where breeders from all over the country compete to establish how well their breeding programmes are developing. A show is also a major social event on the cat calendar.

Whether a potential pet owner or breeder of the future, you should visit one or two shows. It is a great day out for the whole family. Apart from the wonderful selection of breeds, there are also many trade stands. If a product is available, it will be seen at the large exhibitions.

Many of the national clubs and magazines have stands. The two major shows mentioned are held in the winter months, usually November and December. However, there are hundreds of other shows staged during the year in various parts of the country. They range from small local club events to major championship breed shows and are usually advertised in the cat magazines. Your ruling cat association can also supply a list of shows.

SHOW ORGANISATION

So you will have some idea of how things are organised, the following information will be helpful. You will learn even more by purchasing the show catalogue. This contains the names and addresses of the exhibitors and details of their cats. It also lists the prizes, indicates the show regulations, and carries many interesting advertisements.

A major show revolves around three broad categories of cats:
1. Unaltered cats, meaning those that are capable of breeding.
2. Neuters.
3. Non-pedigreed cats.

There is thus the opportunity for every type of cat, from the best of Birmans to the everyday 'moggie' pets, to take part. These three broad categories are divided into various sections. For example, the unaltered and

CLASSES FOR NON-PEDIGREED CATS

For non-pedigreed cats there are many classes which include those for single colours, bicolours, tabbies, half-pedigreed, and so on. In this section are many delightful classes, such as those for cats owned by senior citizens, by young children (by age group), best original stray or rescued cat, best personality, most unusual looking, most photogenic, and best older cats. Within this cat section can be seen some truly gorgeous felines. There is no doubt that the pet classes have been the springboard that has launched many a top breeder into the world of pedigreed cats.

ON THE CONTINENT AND BEYOND...

In Britain, the title of UK Grand Champion or Premier is won in competition with other Grand titleholders. In mainland Europe, cats can become International Champions. More British cats are expected to become International Champions with the recent introduction of passports for cats, allowing cats to compete more freely on the Continent and beyond. In countries other than Britain, the way in which shows are organised and titles achieved do differ somewhat. However, they broadly follow the outline discussed here.

neuters are divided into their respective sections, such as Longhair, Semi-Longhair, British, Foreign, Siamese and so on.

There are many more classes other than those mentioned. These include club classes and those for kittens and non-pedigreed cats.

JUDGING

There are two ways cats can be judged. One is pen judging, the other is bench or ring judging. In Britain pen judging is the normal method, though bench judging is used for Best in Show. In pen judging, the judge moves around the cat pens. The cat gaining the most points when compared to the standard wins. In bench judging, stewards take the cats to the judge.

If a cat wins its class, it then competes against other class winners. By this process of elimination, a cat may go on to win the Best of Breed award. It then competes against other breed winners for the Best in Group award. The group winners compete for the Best in Show award.

A breeder can gather a number of awards during the course of a show. Even those who do not own the very best cats can take pride in gaining second, third, fourth and recommended, especially if won at the larger shows. By progression the top cat at a show will win its class, its breed, its section, and ultimately become the Best in Show exhibit. The titles a cat can win commence with that of Champion, or Premier in the case of neuters. A Grand Champion is made after winning in competition with others of its same status. The same applies to a

Grand Premier. The judging system may vary from one country to another but the basis remains as outlined.

THE SHOW CAT

When a cat is seen preening in its pen, the hard work that has gone into its preparation is rarely appreciated. Exhibits must be in peak condition and their coats in full bloom. The potential exhibit must gradually be trained to spend hours within its show pen. It must display no fear or aggression towards strangers, such as the stewards or the judges. These must be able to physically examine it, including its ears and teeth; it also involves being lifted into the air. If a cat scratches or bites a judge, or any other show official, it is automatically withdrawn from the show. A repeat of this in the future would result, in most instances, in the cat's show career being terminated by the ruling association.

Apart from being comfortable with people peering into its pen, the cat must be able to endure long journeys to the show venue. Unless trained, the cat may become a nervous, aggressive

Show Birmans are content to spend hours in the show pens, a necessity for long days of travelling and exhibiting.

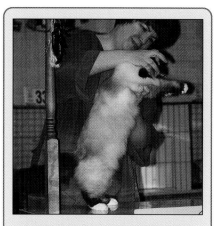

BECOMING AN EXHIBITOR

Before any hobbyist enters a show, he is advised to join a local cat club. Here, hobbyists will meet local breeders who will not only assess their cats for them but also provide help on many other topics. The novice exhibitor could attend one or two shows with an exhibitor in order to learn the ropes. During this period, he can become familiar with the show rules and regulations. These are quite extensive, intended to safeguard the best interests of the hobby, the exhibitors and, most importantly, the cats.

It is of interest to note that some breeders own cats in partnership with other fanciers. This is useful when one person enjoys the breeding and the other the exhibition side. It enables both to really be involved in the hobby to a level that might not have been possible for either on his own. So, whether you fancy being an exhibitor or just love cats, do make a point of visiting the next major show in your area. You may just find the experience addictive!

feline that will have a very short show career.

Obviously the cat must display quality. This means having none of the major faults that would prevent it from gaining a first prize. These are listed in the breed standard. The meaning of quality is very subjective. You do not need to own a potential champion to be a successful exhibitor. The cat must also be registered with the association under whose rules the show is being run. In Britain this will be the Governing Council of the Cat Fancy (GCCF) or The Cat Association of Britain.

As in anything competitive, exhibits can gain prizes at the lower levels of a hobby without having any realistic chance of awards in the major shows. Owning such exhibits is often part of a top breeder/exhibitor's portfolio from their early days in the hobby. Others may never move beyond the smaller shows but still gain reputations for owning sound stock. They thoroughly enjoy being involved at their given level.

If the idea of exhibiting appeals to you, the best way to make a start is to join a local club. There you not only will be advised on all procedures but also will be able to make many new friends. Exhibiting can be costly in cash and time, but you can focus on the more local shows while attending the larger ones as a visitor.

Maintaining a cat in the peak of good health revolves around the implementation of a sound husbandry strategy. At the basic level, this means being responsible about feeding, cleanliness and grooming. However, in spite of an owner's best efforts in these matters, cats may still become ill due to other causes. Although owners can attempt to prevent, identify and react to problems, only a vet is qualified to diagnose and suggest and/or effect remedies. Attempts by owners or 'informed' friends to diagnose and treat for specific diseases are dangerous and potentially life-threatening to the cat.

SELECTING A VETERINARY SURGEON

Your selection of a veterinary surgeon should not be based upon personality (as most are) but upon convenience to your home. You want a vet who is close because you might have emergencies or need to make multiple visits for treatments. You want a vet who has services that you might require such as nail clipping and bathing, as well as sophisticated pet supplies and a good reputation for ability and responsiveness. There is nothing more frustrating than having to wait a day or more to get a response from your veterinary surgeon.

All veterinary surgeons are licensed and their diplomas and/or certificates should be displayed in their waiting rooms. There are, however,

A LONG, HEALTHY LIFE

As veterinary surgeons make medical advances in the health care of cats, the longevity of the typical house cat is improving. Certainly ages between 15 and 18 years are not uncommon, and reports of cats living more than 20 years are predictable.

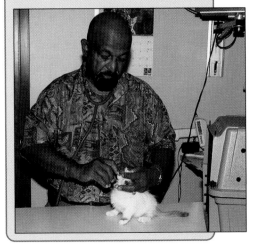

A DELICATE HEART

A cat's heart is as delicate as a human's heart, but it is much smaller. At full maturity, queens' hearts weigh between 9–12 grammes. Toms' hearts are heavier, weighing 11–18 grammes. The blood that circulates through the heart chambers does not supply the heart muscle, thus requiring a separate circulatory system for the heart muscle.

behaviour. Most veterinary surgeons do routine surgery, such as neutering and stitching up wounds. When the problem affecting your cat is serious, it is not unusual or impudent to get another medical opinion, although in Britain you are obliged to advise the vets concerned about this. You might also want to compare costs among several veterinary surgeons. Sophisticated health care and veterinary services can be very costly. It is not infrequent that important decisions are based upon financial considerations.

PREVENTATIVE MEDICINE

It is much easier, less costly and more effective to practise preventative medicine than to fight bouts of illness and disease. Properly bred kittens come from parents who were

many veterinary specialities that usually require further studies and internships. There are specialists in heart problems (veterinary cardiologists), skin problems (veterinary dermatologists), teeth and gum problems (veterinary dentists), eye problems (veterinary ophthalmologists) and x-rays (veterinary radiologists), as well as vets who have specialities in reproduction, nutrition and

THE RIB CAGE

Cats usually have 13 pairs of ribs. The ribs in the middle are longer than the ribs on either end (or beginning) of the rib cage. The first nine ribs are joined to the chest bone (sternum) with costal cartilages. Ribs 10, 11 and 12 are also associated with cartilage, which contributes to the costal arch. The thirteenth rib is called the floating rib and its cartilage is separate from the other ribs.

Birman owners are well advised to find a local vet who is both knowledgeable and caring. A trustworthy vet is vital to your Birman's continued well-being.

TAKE CARE OF THOSE KIDNEYS

The kidney of the cat is larger than that of the dog, but it has the typical bean shape. It receives 25% of the blood output of the heart! For this reason it has rather significant veins to accommodate this large supply of blood, and injuries suffered by the kidneys are usually serious and may be frequent.

selected based upon their genetic disease profile. Their mothers should have been vaccinated, free of all internal and external parasites and properly nourished. For these reasons, a visit to the veterinary surgeon who cared for the queen is recommended. The queen can pass on disease resistance to her kittens, which can last for eight to ten weeks. She can also pass on parasites

and many infections. That's why you should visit the veterinary surgeon who cared for the queen.

VACCINATIONS

Most vaccinations are given by injection and should only be done by a veterinary surgeon. Both he and you should keep a record of the date of the injection, the identification of the vaccine and the amount given. The first vaccination is normally given when the kitten is about 8–9 weeks old. About 30 days later a booster is given. Although there are many diseases to which a cat may fall victim, the most dangerous three—FIE, FVR and FeLV—can

STRESS TEST

Stress reduces the effectiveness of the immune system. Seemingly innocuous conditions may develop into major problems or leave the cat more open to attack by disease. Stress is difficult to specifically identify, but its major causes are well known. These include incorrect diet, intrusion by another cat in its home or territory, excessive handling and petting, disturbed sleep, uncomfortable home temperatures, bullying by another cat or pet, parasitic infestation, boarding in a cattery, travel, moving home, boredom, limited accommodation space and, for some felines, being exhibited.

HEALTH AND VACCINATION SCHEDULE

Age	6 wks	8 wks	10 wks	12 wks	16 wks	6 mos	1 yr
Worm Control	✔	✔	✔		✔		
Neutering						✔	
Rhinotracheitis	✔	✔		✔	✔		✔
Panleukopenia	✔	✔		✔			✔
Calicivirus		✔			✔		✔
Feline Leukaemia				✔			✔
Feline Infectious Peritonitis				✔	✔		✔
Faecal evaluation						✔	
Feline Immunodeficiency testing							✔
Feline Leukaemia testing				✔			✔
Dental evaluation		✔				✔	
Rabies				✔	✔		✔

Vaccinations are not instantly effective. It takes about two weeks for the cat's immunization system to develop antibodies. Most vaccinations require annual booster shots. Your veterinary surgeon should guide you in this regard.

DISEASE REFERENCE CHART

	What is it?	Cause	Symptoms
Feline Leukaemia Virus (FeLV)	Infectious disease; kills more cats each year than any other feline infectious disease.	A virus spread through saliva, tears, urine and faeces of infected cats; bite wounds.	Early on no symptoms may occur, but eventually infected cats experience signs from depression and weight loss to respiratory distress. FelV also suppresses immune system, making a cat susceptible to almost any severe chronic illness.
Rabies	Potentially deadly virus that infects warm-blooded mammals. Not seen in the United Kingdom.	A bacterium, which is often carried by rodents, that enters through mucous membranes and spreads quickly throughout the body.	Aggressiveness, a blank or vacant look in the eyes, increased vocalisation and/or weak or wobbly gait.
Panleukopenia aka Kitty Distemper or Feline Parvovirus	Highly contagious virus, potentially deadly.	Ingestion of the virus, which is usually spread through the faeces of infected cats.	Most common: severe diarrhoea. Also vomiting, fatigue, lack of appetite, severe inflammation of intestines.
Feline Viral Rhinotracheitis (FVR)	Viral disease that affects eyes and upper respiratory tracts.	A virus that can affect any cat, especially those in multiple-cat settings.	Sneezing attacks, coughing, drooling thick saliva, fever, watery eyes, ulcers of mouth, nose and eyes.
Feline Immuno-deficiency Virus (FIV)	Virus that reduces white blood cells.	An infection spread commonly through cat fight wounds.	Signs may be dormant for years or innocuous, such as diarrhoea or anaemia.
Feline Infectious Peritonitis (FIP)	A fatal viral disease, may be linked to FelV and FIV.	Bacteria in dirty litter boxes; stress may increase susceptibility in kittens.	Extremely variable; range from abdominal swelling to chest problems, eye ailments and body lesions.
Feline Urological Syndrome (FUS)	A disease that affects the urinary tracts of cats.	Inflammation of bladder and urethra.	Constipation, constant licking of penis or vulva, blood in urine (males), swollen abdomen, crying when lifted.

be safeguarded against with a single (three-in-one) injection. Thereafter an annual booster is all that is required.

MAJOR DISEASES
There are a number of diseases for which there is either no cure or little chance of recovery. However, some can be prevented by vaccination. All breeders and owners should ensure kittens are so protected.

FELINE INFECTIOUS ENTERITIS (FIE)
This is also known as feline panleukopenia, feline parvovirus and feline distemper. The virus attacks the intestinal system. It is spread via the faeces and urine. The virus may survive for many years in some environments. The use of household bleach (sodium hypochlorite) for cleaning helps to prevent colonisation. Signs, among others, are diarrhoea,

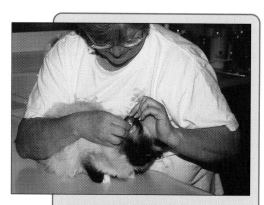

POSSIBLE SOURCES OF EAR PROBLEMS

- Fight scratches
- Excess secretion of wax
- Swellings and blood blisters (haematoma) resulting from intrusion by foreign bodies (grass, etc.)
- Sunburn
- Whitish-coloured ear mites (*Otodectes cynotis*)
- Orange-coloured harvest mites (*Trombicula autumnalis*)
- Fleas
- Bacterial infection of either the outer or middle/inner ear

vomiting, depression, anorexia and dehydration. Death may occur within days. A vaccine is available.

FELINE VIRAL RHINOTRACHEITIS (FVR) & CALICIVIRUS (FCV)

Also known as cat flu, this is a complex of upper respiratory diseases. Signs are excessive hard sneezing, runny nose and mouth ulcers. Cats vaccinated after having contracted flu may recover but may suffer recurrent bouts, especially if they become stressed.

FELINE LEUKAEMIA VIRUS (FeLV)

This is a highly infectious viral disease. It is spread via direct contact—mutual grooming, saliva, feeding bowls, faeces, urine and biting. It can be passed prenatally from a female to her offspring. It creates tumours, anaemia, immune system depression, pyrexia (high temperatures), lethargy, respiratory disease, intestinal disease and many other potentially fatal problems. It is most prevalent in high-density cat populations. Not all cats will be affected, but they may become carriers.

Kittens less than six months old are especially vulnerable. Infected cats usually die by the time they are three to four years old. Cats can be screened or tested for this disease. Vaccination is not 100% effective but is recommended in kittens being sold into multi-cat environments.

FELINE IMMUNODEFICIENCY VIRUS (FIV)

This causes the white blood cells to be significantly reduced, thus greatly suppressing the efficiency of the

By purchasing your Birman kitten from a reputable breeder, you are ensuring that you have a healthy, alert and normal kitten that can become a part of your everyday world.

immune system. It is not transferable to humans. Infection is normally gained from cat-fight wounds; thus, outdoor males are at the most risk. A cat diagnosed via blood tests as FIV-positive may live a normal life for months or years if retained indoors and given careful attention. Signs may be innocuous in the early stages, such as anaemia or diarrhoea. No vaccine is available.

FELINE INFECTIOUS PERITONITIS (FIP)

This viral disease is invariably fatal once contracted in its more potent forms. However, the virulence of the virus is variable and may by destroyed by the immune system. Stress may increase susceptibility in kittens. It may be linked to FeLV and FIV. Signs are extremely variable and range from abdominal swelling to chest problems, eye ailments to body lesions. There are various tests available but none is as yet 100% conclusive. Strict cleanliness is essential, especially of litter trays. No vaccine is available.

FELINE UROLOGICAL SYNDROME (FUS)

This is a very distressing condition caused by an inflammation of the bladder and urethra. Signs are constipation-like squatting and attempts to urinate, regular licking of the penis or vulva, blood in urine (males), swollen abdomen, crying when lifted and urinating in unusual places (often with only small amounts).

The numerous causes include infection, dirty litter tray of the indoor cat, alkaline urine (in cats it should be acidic), diet too dry, lack of water intake (even though this may be available) and being hit by a vehicle (damaged nerves). Veterinary treatment is essential or the condition could be fatal due to the bladder bursting or

HEALTHY CAT

There are more cats than dogs. This has stimulated the veterinary medical community to learn more about cats and to prescribe more modern medicines to keep felines healthier.

Although your Birman kitten weighs little in poundage, it is a hefty responsibility to bear.

the presence of dangerous bacteria.

RABIES

Britain and most European Community countries are free of this terrible disease. The stringent quarantine laws of Britain are such that vaccination is not necessary. However, the introduction of passports for dogs and cats means that resident British cats must be vaccinated if they are to travel abroad and return to the UK without being placed into quarantine. The vaccination is given when the kitten is three or more months old. The pet passport process takes at least six months to complete, so plan well ahead.

COMMON HEALTH PROBLEMS

DERMATITIS (ECZEMA)

Dry, lifeless coat, loss of coat, tiny scabs over the head and body, loose flakes (dandruff) and excessive scratching are all

NEUTERING

Neutering is a major means of avoiding ill health. It dramatically reduces the risk of males becoming involved in territorial battles with the dangers of physical injury and disease transference. It makes the male more placid and less likely to scent mark its home. It also reduces the incidence of prostate problems and there is no risk of testicular cancer. The female avoids potentially lethal illnesses related to her being allowed to remain in an unmated condition, such as breast cancer.

Neutering is usually performed between six and four months of age but it can be done as early as eight weeks of age. Data available on the age at which a kitten is neutered indicate that early neutering has more advantages than drawbacks. Breeders should have this performed on all cats sold as pets.

Male cats are neutered. The operation removes the testicles and requires that the cat be anaesthetised. Females are spayed. This is a major surgery during which the ovaries and uterus are removed. Both males and females should be kept quiet at home for about seven to ten days following the procedure, at which time the vet will remove the sutures.

commonly called eczema. The cause covers a range of possibilities including diet, parasitic mites such as *Cheyletiella spp.*, fungus or an allergy to flea or other bites. Sometimes reasons are unknown. Veterinary diagnosis and treatment are required.

RINGWORM (DERMATOPHYTOSIS)

This problem is fungal, not that of a worm. The most common form is *Microsporum canis*, which accounts for over 90% of cases. Cats less than one year old are at the highest risk, while longhaired breeds are more prone to the problem than shorthaired cats. The fungi feed on the keratin layers of the skin, nails and hair. Direct contact and spores that remain in the environment are the main means of transmission.

Typical signs are circular-type bald areas of skin, which may be flaked and reddish. The coat generally may become dry and lifeless, giving the appearance of numerous other skin and hair problems. Veterinary diagnosis and treatment, either topical or via drugs, is essential as the condition is zoonotic, meaning it can be transferred to humans.

EAR PROBLEMS

Most of the common ear problems affect the outer ear.

BLOOD GROUP INCOMPATIBILITY (BGI)

In recent years blood group incompatibility has become the focus of scientists, vets and breeders. Its importance to pet owners is when transfusions are needed. For breeders it probably accounts for a large percentage of kittens that die from fading kitten syndrome. Scientifically the problem is called neonatal erythrolysis, meaning the destruction of red blood cells in newly born offspring.

Cats have two blood groups, A & B. Group A is dominant to B (which is genetically called recessive). When the antibodies of B group mothers are passed to A group kittens, via her colostrum milk, they destroy red blood cells. Death normally follows within a few days.

Most domestic cats tested are group A. However, national and regional differences display a variation in which 1-6% may be of type B. In pedigreed breeds it has been found that the number of group B cats varies significantly. The following breeds, based on present available data, have the indicated percentage incidence of group B blood type.

0%	Siamese, Burmese and Oriental Shorthair
1-5%	Maine Coon, Manx and Norwegian Forest
10-20%	Abyssinian, Birman, Japanese Bobtail, Persian, Scottish Fold and Somali
25-50%	British Shorthair, Devon and Cornish Rex and Exotic Shorthair

The clear implication to breeders is to establish their cats' blood group, via testing, and conduct appropriate matings. These should not result in B group mothers nursing A group kittens. The safe matings are:

1. Group A males   x   A females
2. Group B males   x   A or B females
3. Group A females   x   A or B males
4. Group B females   x   B males

Breeders are advised to seek further information before embarking on stock purchase and breeding programmes.

The telltale sign is the cat's constant scratching of the ears and/or its holding the ear to one side. Greasy hairs around the ear, dark brown wax (cerumen) in the ears, scaly flakes in or around the ear or minute white or orange pinhead-like bodies (mites) in the ear are common signs. Canker is a term used for ear infections, but it has no specific meaning.

Over-the-counter remedies for ear problems are ineffective unless correct diagnosis has been made. It is therefore better to let the vet diagnose and treat the cat. Some problems may require anaesthesia and minor surgery.

DIARRHOEA
This is a general term used to indicate a semi-liquid to liquid

KEEPING YOUR CAT HEALTHY
Although there are a multitude of ailments, diseases and accidents that could befall a cat, all but the most minor of problems can be avoided with good management. The following tips are a recipe for keeping your cat in the peak of health.

• Make sure it is vaccinated and in other ways protected from each of the major diseases. It must also receive annual boosters to maintain immunity.
• Have periodic checks made by your vet to see if your cat has worms.
• Ensure the cat receives an adequate diet that is both appealing and balanced.
• Have the kitten neutered if it is not to be used for breeding.
• Ensure the cat's litter tray, food/water vessels and grooming tools are always maintained in spotless condition.
• Do not let your cat out overnight or when you are away working or shopping.
• Always wash your hands after gardening or petting other people's pets.
• Groom your cat daily. If this is done, you will more readily notice fleas or other problems than if grooming was done less frequently.
• Never try to diagnose and treat problems that are clearly of an internal type. Remember, even the most informed of breeders is not a vet and unable to reliably diagnose problems for you or suggest treatments. Contact your vet.
• If you are ever in doubt about the health of your cat, do not delay in discussing your concerns with your vet. Delays merely allow problems to become more established.

state of faecal matter. Mild to acute cases may be due to a change of environment, dietary change, eating an 'off' item, gorging on a favoured food, stress or a minor chill. These often rectify themselves within days. Chronic and persistent diarrhoea may be the result of specific diseases. Any indication of blood in the faecal matter must be considered dangerous.

In minor cases, withholding food for 12–24 hours, or feeding a simple diet, may arrest the condition. If not, contact your vet. Faecal analysis and blood testing may be required. By answering numerous questions related to the cat's diet, general health, level of activity, loss of appetite, etc., the vet will determine whether tests are required or if immediate treatment is warranted. Do not give cats human or canine intestinal remedies; these could prove dangerous.

CONSTIPATION

When a cat strains but is unable to pass motions, this is indicative of various causes. It may have hairballs, may have eaten a bird or rodent and has a bone lodged in its intestinal tract, may be suffering from a urological problem rather than constipation, or may have been hit by a car and has damaged the nerves that control bowel movements. As constipation is potentially serious, veterinary advice should be sought. Laxatives and faecal softener tablets may be given, the faecal matter can be surgically removed or another treatment carried out.

CLEANLINESS IS THE KEY
Crucial to the prevention and spread of disease is the need to maintain meticulous cleanliness, especially relating to the litter tray. Many diseases and problems are transferred via faecal matter. Once a problem is suspected, the advice of a vet should be sought. Blood tests, faecal microscopy and other testing methods are now available. They can make the difference between life and death for a cherished pet.

EXTERNAL PARASITES

FLEAS

Of all the problems to which cats are prone, none is more well-known and frustrating than fleas. Indeed, flea-related problems are the principal cause of visits to veterinary surgeons. Flea infestation is relatively simple to cure but difficult to prevent. Periodic flea checks for your cat, conducted as well as annual health check-ups, are highly recommended. Consistent dosing with anthelmintic preparations is also advised. Parasites that are harboured inside the body are a bit more difficult to eradicate but they are easier to control.

To control a flea infestation you have to understand the flea's life cycle. Fleas are often thought of as a summertime problem but centrally heated homes have changed the life-cycle patterns, and fleas can be found at any time of the year. Fleas thrive in hot and humid environments; they soon die if the temperature drops below 35°F. The most effective method of flea control is a two-stage approach: one stage to kill the adult fleas, and the other to control the development of pre-adult fleas. Unfortunately, no

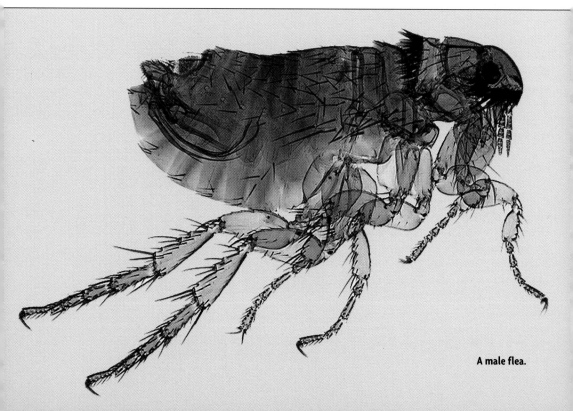

A male flea.

single active ingredient is effective against all stages of the life cycle.

LIFE CYCLE STAGES
During its life, a flea will pass through four life stages: egg, larva, pupa and adult. The adult stage is the most visible and irritating stage of the flea life cycle, and this is why the majority of flea-control products concentrates on this stage. The fact is that adult fleas account for only 1% of the total flea population, and the other 99% exist in pre-adult stages, i.e. eggs, larvae and pupae. The pre-adult stages are barely visible to the naked eye.

THE LIFE CYCLE OF THE FLEA
Eggs are laid on the cat, usually in quantities of about 20 or 30, several times a day. The female adult flea must have a blood meal before each egg-laying session. When first laid, the eggs will not cling to the cat's fur, as the eggs are not sticky. They will immediately fall to the floor or ground, especially if the cat moves around or scratches.

Once the eggs fall from the cat onto the carpet or furniture, they will hatch into yellow larvae, approximately 2 mms long. This takes from 5 to 11 days. Larvae are not particularly mobile, and

A Look at Fleas

Fleas have been around for millions of years and have adapted to changing host animals. They are able to go through a complete life cycle in less than one month or they can extend their lives to almost two years by remaining as pupae or cocoons. They must have a blood meal every 10-14 days, and egg production begins within two days of their first meal. The female cat flea is very prolific and can lay 2000 eggs in her lifetime!

Fleas have been measured as being able to jump 300,000 times and can jump 150 times their length in any direction, including straight up. Those are just a few of the reasons why they are so successful in infesting a cat!

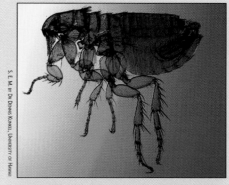

A scanning electron micrograph (S. E. M.) of a flea.

S. E. M. BY DR DENNIS KUNKEL, UNIVERSITY OF HAWAII

Magnified head of a flea.

S. E. M. BY DR DENNIS KUNKEL, UNIVERSITY OF HAWAII

will usually travel only a few inches from where they hatch. However, they do have a tendency to move away from light and heavy traffic—under furniture, in the carpet and behind doors are common places to find high quantities of flea larvae.

The flea larvae feed on dead organic matter, including adult flea faeces, until they are ready to change into adult fleas. Fleas will usually remain as larvae for around seven days, becoming darker in colour. After this period, the larvae will pupate a protective cocoon. While inside the pupae, the larvae will undergo metamorphosis and change into adult fleas. This can happen within a week, but the adult fleas can remain inside the pupae waiting to hatch for up to six months. The pupae are signalled to hatch by certain stimuli, such as physical pressure—the pupae's being stepped on, heat from an animal lying on the pupae or increased carbon dioxide levels and vibrations—indicating that a suitable host is available.

> **DID YOU KNOW?**
> Never mix flea control products without first consulting your veterinary surgeon. Some products can become toxic when combined with others and can cause serious or fatal consequences.

> **DID YOU KNOW?**
> Flea-killers are poisonous. You should not spray these toxic chemicals on areas of a cat's body that he licks, on his genitals or on his face. Flea killers taken internally are a better answer, but check with your vet in case internal therapy is not advised for your cat.

Once hatched, the adult flea must feed within a few days. Once the adult flea finds a host, it will not leave voluntarily. It only becomes dislodged by grooming or the host animal's scratching. The adult flea will remain on the host for the duration of its life unless forcibly removed.

TREATING THE ENVIRONMENT AND THE CAT

Treating fleas should be a two-pronged attack. First, the environment needs to be treated; this includes carpets and furniture, especially the cat's bedding and areas underneath furniture. The environment should be treated with a household spray containing an Insect Growth Regulator (IGR) and an insecticide to kill the adult fleas. There are also liquids, given orally, that contain chitin inhibitors. These render flea eggs incapable of development. There are both foam and liquid wipe-on treatments. Additionally, cats can

Opposite page: A scanning electron micrograph of a flea magnified more than 100x. This image has been colorized for effect.

The Life Cycle of the Flea

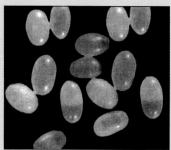
Eggs

Larva

Pupa

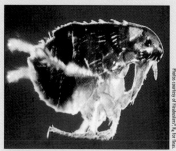
Adult

Photos courtesy of Fleabusters® R₂ for fleas.

Flea Control

IGR (INSECT GROWTH REGULATOR)

Two types of products should be used when treating fleas—a product to treat the pet and a product to treat the home. Adult fleas represent less than 1% of the flea population. The pre-adult fleas (eggs, larvae and pupae) represent more than 99% of the flea population and are found in the environment; it is in the case of pre-adult fleas that products containing an Insect Growth Regulator (IGR) should be used in the home.

IGRs are a new class of compounds used to prevent the development of insects. They do not kill the insect outright, but instead use the insect's biology against it to stop it from completing its growth. Products that contain methoprene are the world's first and leading IGRs. Used to control fleas and other insects, this type of IGR will stop flea larvae from developing and protect the house for up to seven months.

EN GARDE:
CATCHING FLEAS OFF GUARD!

Consider the following ways to arm yourself against fleas:

• Add a small amount of pennyroyal or eucalyptus oil to your cat's bath. These natural remedies repel fleas.
• Supplement your cat's food with fresh garlic (minced or grated) and a hearty amount of brewer's yeast, both of which ward off fleas.
• Use a flea comb on your cat daily. Submerge fleas in a cup of bleach to kill them quickly.
• Confine the cat to only a few rooms to limit the spread of fleas in the home.
• Vacuum daily...and get all of the crevices! Dispose of the bag every few days until the problem is under control.
• Wash your cat's bedding daily. Cover cushions where your cat sleeps with towels, and wash the towels often.

be injected with treatments that can last up to six months. Emulsions that have the same effect can also be added to food. The advanced treatments are only available from veterinary surgeons. The IGRs actually mimic the fleas' own hormones and stop the eggs and larvae from developing into adult fleas. There are currently no treatments available to attack the pupa stage of the life cycle, so the adult insecticide is used to kill the newly hatched adult fleas before they find a host. Most IGRs are active for many months, while adult insecticides are only active for a few days.

When treating with a household spray, it is a good idea to vacuum before applying the product. This stimulates as many pupae as possible to hatch into adult fleas. The vacuum cleaner should also be treated with a flea treatment to prevent the eggs and larvae that have been hoovered into the vacuum bag from hatching.

The second stage of treatment is to apply an adult insecticide to the cat, usually in the form of a collar or a spray. Alternatively, there are drops that, when placed on the back of the animal's neck, spread throughout the fur and skin to kill adult fleas. A word of warning: Never use products sold for dogs on your cat; the result could be fatal.

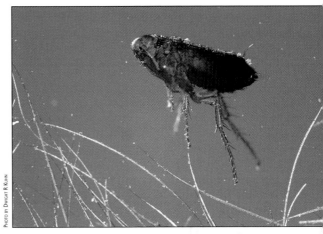

Dwight R Kuhn's magnificent action photo showing a flea jumping.

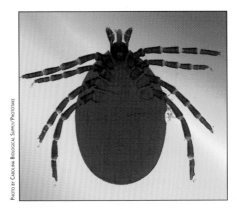

A brown tick, *Rhipicephalus sanguineus*, is an uncommon but annoying tick found on cats.

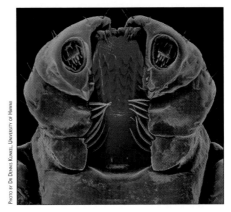

The head of a tick, *Dermacentor variabilis*, enlarged and coloured for effect.

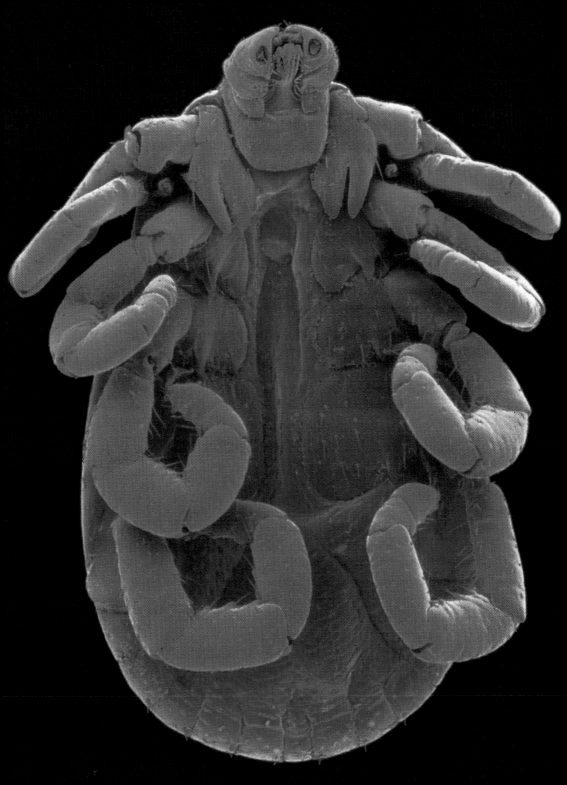

TICKS AND MITES

Though not as common as fleas, ticks and mites are found all over the tropical and temperate world. They don't bite, like fleas; they harpoon. They dig their sharp proboscis (nose) into the cat's skin and drink the blood. Their only food and drink is cat's blood. Cats can get potentially fatal anaemias, paralysis and many other diseases from ticks and mites. They may live where fleas are found and they like to hide in cracks or seams in walls wherever cats live. They are controlled the same way fleas are controlled.

The *Dermacentor variabilis* may well be the most common tick in many geographical areas, especially those areas where the climate is hot and humid. The other common ticks that attack small animals are *Rhipicephalus sanguineus*, *Ixodes* and some species of *Amblyomma*.

Most ticks have life expectancies of a week to six months, depending upon climatic conditions. They can neither jump nor fly, but they can crawl slowly and can range up to 5 metres (16 feet) to reach a sleeping or unsuspecting animal.

INTERNAL PARASITES

Most animals—fishes, birds and mammals, including cats and humans—have worms and other parasites that live inside their bodies. According to Dr Herbert R Axelrod, the fish pathologist, there are two kinds of parasites: dumb and smart. The smart parasites live in peaceful cooperation with their

TOXOPLASMOSIS AND PREGNANT WOMEN

Toxoplasmosis is caused by a single parasite, *Toxoplasma gondii*. Cats acquire it by eating infected prey, such as rodents or birds, or raw meat. Obviously, strictly indoor cats are at less risk of infection than cats that are permitted to roam outdoors. Symptoms include diarrhoea, listlessness, pneumonia and inflammation of the eye. Sometimes there are no symptoms. The disease can be treated with antibiotics.

The only way humans can get the disease is through direct contact with the cat's faeces. People usually don't display any symptoms, although they can show mild flu-like symptoms. Once exposed, an antibody is produced and the person builds immunity to the disease. The real danger to humans is that pregnant women can pass the parasite to the developing foetus. In this case the chances are good that the baby will be born with a major health problem and/or serious birth defects. In order to eliminate risk, pregnant women should have someone else deal with the litter-box duties or wear gloves while taking care of the litter box and wash hands thoroughly afterwards.

Opposite page: The tick, *Dermacentor variabilis*, is one of the most common ticks found on cats. Look at the strength in its eight legs! No wonder it's hard to detach them.

INTERNAL PARASITES OF CATS

NAME	DESCRIPTION	SYMPTOMS	ACQUISTION	TREATMENT
Roundworm (*Toxocara cati* and *Toxascaris leonina*)	Large white coil-like worms 2–4 inches long, resembling small springs.	Vomiting, pot belly, respiratory problems, poor growth rate, protruding third eyelids, poor hair coat.	Ingesting infective larvae; ingesting infected mammals, birds or insects; a queen with *Toxocari cati* nursing kittens.	Anthelmintics; scrupulously clean environment (e.g. daily removal of all faeces recommended).
***Physaloptera* species**	1–6 inches long, attacks the wall of the stomach.	Vomiting, anorexia, melena.	Eating insects that live in soil (e.g. May Beetles).	Diagnosed with a gastroscope—treated with pyrantel pamoate. Prevention of exposure to the intermediate hosts.
***Gordius* or Horsehair worm**	6-inch pale brown worms with stripes.	Vomiting.	May ingest a worm while drinking from or contact with swimming pools and toilet bowls.	Anthelmintics; avoiding potentially infected environments.
Hookworm (*Ancylostoma tubaeforme*)	The adult worms, ranging from 6 to 15 mm in length, attach themselves to the small intestines.	Anemia, melena, weight loss, poor hair coat.	Larva penetrating the cat's skin, usually attacks the small intestine. Found in soil and flower gardens where feacal matter is deposited.	Fortnightly treatment with anthelmintics. Good sanitation (e.g. daily cleanup of litter boxes).
Tapeworm (*Dipylidium caninum* and *Taenia taeniformis*)	Up to 3 feet long. Parts shaped similar to cucumber seeds. The most common intermediate hosts are fleas and biting lice.	No clinical signs—difficult to detect.	Eating injected adult fleas. Uses rodents as hosts.	Praziquantel and epsiprantel. Management of environment to ensure scrupulously clean conditions. Proper flea control.

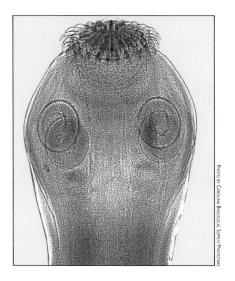

PHOTO BY CAROLINA BIOLOGICAL SUPPLY/PHOTOTAKE

DEWORMING

Ridding your kitten of worms is VERY IMPORTANT because certain worms that kittens carry, such as tapeworms and roundworms, can infect humans.

Breeders initiate a deworming programme at or about four weeks of age. The routine is repeated every two or three weeks until the kitten is three months old. The breeder from whom you obtained your kitten should provide you with the complete details of the deworming programme.

Your veterinary surgeon can prescribe and monitor the programme of deworming for you. The usual programme is treating the kitten every 15–20 days until the kitten is positively worm-free.

It is advised that you only treat your kitten with drugs that are recommended professionally.

hosts (symbiosis), while the dumb parasites kill their host. Most of the worm infections are relatively easy to control. If they are not controlled, they weaken the host cat to the point that other medical problems occur, but they are not dumb parasites.

HOOKWORMS

The worm *Ancylostoma tubaeforme* can inject a cat by larva penetrating its skin. It attaches itself to the small intestine of the cat, where it sucks blood. This loss of blood could cause iron-deficiency anaemia.

Outdoor cats that spend much of their time in the garden or in contact with soil are commonly injected with hookworm. There is another worm, the *Gordius* or horsehair worm, that, if ingested by cat, causes vomiting.

TAPEWORMS

There are many species of tapeworms. They are carried by fleas! The cat eats the flea and starts the tapeworm cycle. Humans can also be infected with tapeworms, so don't eat fleas! Fleas are so small that your cat could pass them onto your hands, your plate or your food and thus make it possible for you to ingest a flea that is carrying tapeworm eggs.

While tapeworm infection is

Magnified heartworm larvae, *Dirofilaria immitis.*

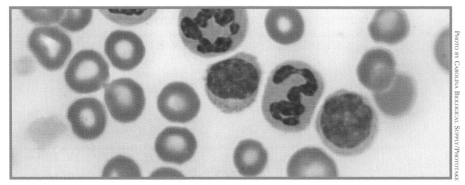

PHOTO BY CAROLINA BIOLOGICAL SUPPLY/PHOTOTAKE

The heartworm, *Dirofilaria immitis.*

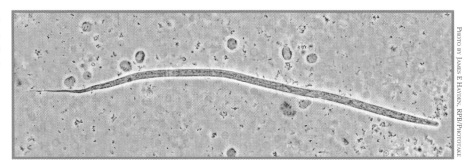

PHOTO BY JAMES F. HAYDEN, RPB/PHOTOTAKE

not life-threatening in cats (smart parasite!), it can be the cause of a very serious liver disease for humans. About 50 percent of the humans infected with *Echinococcus multilocularis*, a type of tapeworm that causes alveolar hydatis, perish.

HEARTWORMS

Heartworms are thin, extended worms up to 30 cms (12 ins) long, which are difficult to diagnose in cats as the worms are too few to be identified by the antigen-detection test. Symptoms may be loss of energy, loss of appetite, coughing, the development of a pot belly and anaemia. Heartworm injection in cats should be treated very seriously as it is often fatal.

Heartworms are transmitted by mosquitoes. The mosquito drinks the blood of an infected cat and takes in larvae with the blood. It takes two to three weeks for the larvae to develop to the infective stage within the body of the mosquito. Cats are less frequently infected with heartworms than dogs are. Also, the parasite is more likely to attack the cat's brain or other organs rather than the heart. Cats should be treated at about six weeks of age, and maintained on a prophylactic dose given monthly.

First Aid at a Glance

BURNS/SCALDS
Place the affected area under cool water; use ice if only a small area is burnt. Do not cover the burn or clip hair away. Petroleum jelly can be applied; take cat to vet immediately.

CHEMICAL BURNS
Wash with water only. If you know the chemical is acid, a weak solution of sodium bicarbonate will help, or a vinegar solution will do for alkaline burns.

BEE/INSECT BITES
Apply freshly sliced onion. Apply ice to relieve swelling; antihistamine dosed properly.

AUTOMOBILE ACCIDENT
Move cat from roadway with blanket; seek veterinary aid.

ANIMAL BITES
Clean any bleeding area; apply pressure until bleeding subsides; go to the vet.

SHOCK
Calm the cat, keep him warm and in a horizontal position; seek immediate veterinary aid.

SPIDER BITES
Use cold compress and a pressurised pack to inhibit venom's spreading.

NOSEBLEED
Apply cold compress to the nose; apply pressure to any visible abrasion.

ANTIFREEZE POISONING
Induce vomiting with hydrogen peroxide. Seek *immediate* veterinary help!

BLEEDING
Apply pressure above the area; treat wound by applying a cotton pack.

FISH HOOKS
Removal best handled by vet; hook must be cut in order to remove.

HEAT STROKE
Move animal to cool, shaded area, wet animal with water and place ice packs around head and body; seek immediate veterinary aid.

SNAKE BITES
Pack ice around bite; contact vet quickly; identify snake for proper antivenin.

FROSTBITE/HYPOTHERMIA
Warm the cat with a warm bath, electric blankets or hot water bottles.

ASPHYXIA
Cat must breathe fresh air as soon as possible. Encourage your cat to move around.

ABRASIONS
Clean the wound and wash out thoroughly with fresh water; apply antiseptic.

Remember: an injured cat may attempt to bite a helping hand from fear and confusion. Handle your cat in a calm and gentle manner so as to avoid upsetting the animal further.

THE GERIATRIC CAT

Depending on lifestyle, most cats are considered old at 12 years of age. Some problems that are associated with cats in their senior years are:

- Decreased energy
- Intolerance to heat and cold
- Less meticulous grooming and litter-box habits
- Decrease in mental alertness
- Decline of liver and kidney functions
- Greater susceptibility to diseases, especially dental disease
- Increased occurrence of cancer

As long as owners pay attention and adjust for changing behaviour and diet, and continue regular veterinary care, cats can live well into their teens—some even 20 years and older!

WHAT TO DO WHEN THE TIME COMES

You are never fully prepared to make a rational decision about putting your cat to sleep. It is very obvious that you love your cat or you would not be reading this book. Putting a loved cat to sleep is extremely difficult. It is a decision that must be made with your veterinary surgeon. You are usually forced to make the decision when your beloved pet will only suffer more and experience no enjoyment for the balance of its life. Then euthanasia is the right choice.

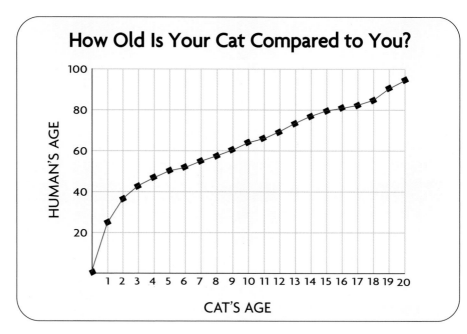

How Old Is Your Cat Compared to You?

What Is Euthanasia?

Euthanasia derives from the Greek meaning *good death*. In other words, it means the planned, painless killing of a cat suffering from a painful, incurable condition, or who is so aged that it cannot walk, see, eat or control its excretory functions.

Euthanasia is usually accomplished by injection with an overdose of an anaesthesia or barbiturate. Aside from the prick of the needle, the experience is usually painless.

Making the Decision

The decision to euthanise your cat is never easy. The days during which the cat becomes ill and the end occurs can be unusually stressful for you. If this is your first experience with the death of a loved one, you may need the comfort dictated by your religious beliefs. If you are the head of the family and have children, you should have involved them in the decision of putting your cat to sleep. Usually your cat can be maintained on drugs for a few days in order to give you ample time to make a decision. During this time, talking with members of your family or even people who have lived through this same experience can ease the burden of your inevitable decision.

The Final Resting Place

Cats can have some of the same privileges as humans. The remains of your beloved cat can be buried in a pet cemetery, which is generally expensive. Cats who have died at home can be buried in your garden in a place suitably marked with some stone or newly planted tree or bush. Alternatively, they can be cremated individually and the ashes returned to you. A less expensive option is mass cremation, although, of course, the ashes can not then be returned. Vets can usually arrange the cremation on your behalf. The cost of these options should always be discussed frankly and openly with your veterinary surgeon.

The remains of your beloved cat can be buried in a pet cemetery.

HOMEOPATHY:

an alternative to conventional medicine

'Less is Most'

Using this principle, the strength of a homeopathic remedy is measured by the number of serial dilutions that were undertaken to create it. The greater the number of serial dilutions, the greater the strength of the homeopathic remedy. The potency of a remedy that has been made by making a dilution of 1 part in 100 parts (or 1/100) is 1c or 1cH. If this remedy is subjected to a series of further dilutions, each one being 1/100, a more dilute and stronger remedy is produced. If the remedy is diluted in this way six times, it is called 6c or 6cH. A dilution of 6c is 1 part in 1000,000,000,000. In general, higher potencies in more frequent doses are better for acute symptoms and lower potencies in more infrequent doses are more useful for chronic, long-standing problems.

CURING OUR CATS NATURALLY

Holistic medicine means treating the whole animal as a unique, perfect living being. Generally, holistic treatments do not suppress the symptoms that the body naturally produces, as do most medications prescribed by conventional doctors and vets. Holistic methods seek to cure disease by regaining balance and harmony in the patient's environment. Some of these methods include use of nutritional therapy, herbs, flower essences, aromatherapy, acupuncture, massage, chiropractic, and, of course the most popular holistic approach, homeopathy. Homeopathy is a theory or system of treating illness with small doses of substances which, if administered in larger quantities, would produce the symptoms that the patient already has. This approach is often described as 'like cures like.' Although modern veterinary medicine is geared toward the 'quick fix,' homeopathy relies on the belief that, given the time, the body is able to heal itself and return to its natural, healthy state.

Choosing a remedy to cure a problem in our cats is the difficult part of homeopathy. Consult with your veterinary surgeon for a professional diagnosis of your cat's symptoms. Often these symptoms require immediate conventional care. If your vet is willing and knowledgeable, you may attempt a homeopathic remedy. Be aware that cortisone prevents homeopathic remedies from working. There are hundreds of possibilities and combinations to cure many problems in cats, from basic physical problems such as excessive moulting, fleas or other parasites, fever, severe skin problems, upset tummy, dry, oily or dull coat, diarrhoea, ear problems or eye discharge (including tears and dry or mucousy matter), to behavioural abnormalities, such as fear of loud noises, hypersensitivity to pain, poor appetite, aversion to touch, obesity and various phobias. From alumina to zincum metallicum, the remedies span the planet and the imagination…from flowers and weeds to chemicals, insect droppings, table salt and volcanic ash.

Using 'Like to Treat Like'

Unlike conventional medicines that suppress symptoms, homeopathic remedies treat illnesses with small doses of substances that, if administered in larger quantities, would produce the symptoms that the patient already has. While the same homeopathic remedy can be used to treat different symptoms in different cats, here are some interesting remedies and their uses.

Apis Mellifica
(made from honey bee venom) can be used for allergies or to reduce swelling that occurs in acutely infected kidneys.

Calcarea Fluorica
(made from calcium fluoride which helps harden bone structure) can be useful in treating hard lumps in tissues.

Kali Muriaticum
(made from potassium chloride) can help improve sluggish behaviour.

Natrum Muriaticum
(made from common salt, sodium chloride) is useful in treating thin, thirsty cats.

Nitricum Acidum
(made from nitric acid) is used for symptoms you would expect to see from contact with acids such as lesions, especially where the skin joins the linings of body orifices or openings such as the lips and nostrils.

Symphytum
(made from the herb Knitbone, Symphytum officianale) is used to encourage bones to heal.

Urtica Urens
(made from the common stinging nettle) is used in treating painful, irritating rashes.

HOMEOPATHIC REMEDIES FOR YOUR CAT

Symptom/Ailment	Possible Remedy
ABSCESSES	Ferrum Phosphoricum 1.5c, Ledum 1.5c, Echinacea Angustifolia, Silicea 3c
ALLERGIES	Apis Mellifica 30c, Astacus Fluviatilis 6c, Pulsatilla 30c, Urtica Urens 6c
ALOPECIA	Alumina 30c, Lycopodium 30c, Sepia 30c, Thallium 6c
BLADDER PROBLEMS	Thlaspi Bursa Pastoris, Urtica Urens 3c, Apis Mellifica 1.5c, Rhus Toxicodendron 3c
CONSTIPATION	Alumina 6c, Carbo Vegetabilis 30c, Graphites 6c, Nitricum Acidum 30c, Silicea 6c
COUGHING	Aconitum Napellus 6c, Belladonna 30c, Hyoscyamus Niger 30c, Phosphorus 30c
DIARRHOEA	Arsenicum Album 30c, Aconitum Napellus 6c, Chamomilla 30c, Mercurius Corrosivus 30c
DRY EYE	Zincum Metallicum 30c
EAR MITES	Thyme (Thymus Vulgaris), Rosemary (Rosemarinus Officinalis), Rue (Ruta Gravedens)
EAR PROBLEMS	Aconitum Napellus 30c, Belladonna 30c, Hepar Sulphuris 30c, Tellurium 30c, Psorinum 200c
EYE PROBLEMS	Borax 6c, Aconitum Napellus 30c, Graphites 6c, Staphysagria 6c, Thuja Occidentalis 30c
FVR (Feline Viral Rhinotracheitis)	Ferrum Phosphoricum 3c, Kali Muriaticum 3c, Natrum Muriaticum 3c, Calcarea Phosphorica 3c
GLAUCOMA	Aconitum Napellus 30c, Apis Mellifica 6c, Phosphorus 30c
HEAT STROKE	Belladonna 30c, Gelsemium Sempervirens 30c, Sulphur 30c
HICCOUGHS	Cinchona Deficinalis 6c
INCONTINENCE	Argentum Nitricum 6c, Causticum 30c, Conium Maculatum 30c, Pulsatilla 30c, Sepia 30c
INSECT BITES	Apis Mellifica 30c, Cantharis 30c, Hypericum Perforatum 6c, Urtica Urens 30c
ITCHING	Alumina 30c, Arsenicum Album 30c, Carbo Vegetabilis 30c, Hypericum Perforatum 6c, Mezerium 6c, Sulphur 30c
LIVER PROBLEMS	Natrum Sulphuricum 1.5c, Bryonia 3c
MASTITIS	Apis Mellifica 30c, Belladonna 30c, Urtica Urens 1m
PENIS PROBLEMS	Aconitum Napellus 30c, Hepar Sulphuris Calcareum 30c, Pulsatilla 30c, Thuja Occidentalis 6c
RINGWORM	Plantago Major, Hydrastis Canadensis, Lavendula Vera, Sulphur 3c
UNDERWEIGHT CATS	Medicago Sativa, Calcarea Phosphorica 3c
VOMITING	Ipecac Root 1.5c, Ferrum Phosphoricum 3c

Recognising a Sick Cat

Unlike colicky babies and cranky children, our feline charges cannot tell us when they are feeling ill. Therefore, there are a number of signs that owners can identify to know that their cats are not feeling well.

Take note for physical manifestations such as:

- unusual, bad odour, including bad breath
- excessive moulting
- wax in the ears, chronic ear irritation
- oily, flaky, dull haircoat
- mucous, tearing or similar discharge in the eyes
- fleas or mites
- mucous in stool, diarrhoea
- sensitivity to petting or handling
- licking at paws, scratching face, etc.

Keep an eye out for behavioural changes as well including:

- lethargy, idleness
- lack of patience or general irritability
- lack of appetite, digestive problems
- phobias (fear of people, loud noises, etc.)
- strange behaviour, suspicion, fear
- coprophagia
- whimpering, crying

Get Well Soon

You don't need a DVR or a BVMA to provide good TLC to your sick or recovering cat, but you do need to pay attention to some details that normally wouldn't bother him. The following tips will aid Kitty's recovery and get him back on his paws again:

- Keep his space free of irritating smells, like heavy perfumes and air fresheners.
- Rest is the best medicine! Avoid harsh lighting that will prevent your cat from sleeping. Shade him from bright sunlight during the day and dim the lights in the evening.
- Keep the noise level down. Animals are more sensitive to sound when they are sick.

- Be attentive to any necessary temperature adjustments. A cat with a fever needs a cool room and cold liquids. A queen that is birthing or recovering from surgery will be more comfortable in a warm room, consuming warm liquids and food.
- You wouldn't send a sick child back to school early, so don't rush your cat back into a full routine until he seems absolutely ready.

USEFUL ADDRESSES

GREAT BRITAIN
The Governing Council of the Cat Fancy (GCCF)
4-6 Penel Orlieu, Bridgewater, Somerset, TA6 3PG
Email: GCCF_CATS@compuserve.com Fax: 01278 446627 Tel: 01278 427575

The Cat Association of Britain (CA)
Mill House, Letcombe Regis, Oxon OX12 9JD   Tel: 01235-766-543

EUROPE
Federation Internationale Feline (FIFe)
Little Dene, Lenham Heath, Maidstone, Kent ME17 2BS, GB
Email: penbyd@compuserve.com   Fax: 1622 850193 Tel: 1622 850908

World Cat Federation (WCF)
Hubertsrabe 280, D-45307, Essen, Germany
Email: wcf@nrw-online.de   Fax: 201-552747 Tel: 201-555724

AUSTRALIA
The Australian Cat Federation, Inc. (ACF)
PO Box 3305, Port Adelaide, SA 5015
Email: acf@catlover.com   Fax: 08 8242 2767 Tel: 08 8449 5880

CANADA
Canadian Cat Association (CCA)
220 Advance Boulevard, Suite 101, Brampton, Ontario L6T 4J5
Email: office@cca-afc.com   Fax: 99050 459-4023 Tel: 99060459-1481

SOUTH AFRICA
Cat Federation of Southern Africa (CFSA)
PO Box 25, Bromhof 2154, Gauteng Province, Republic of South Africa

USA
American Cat Association (ACA)
8101 Katherine Avenue, Panorama City, CA 91402
Fax: (818) 781-5340 Tel: (818) 781-5656

American Cat Fanciers Association
PO Box 203, Point Lookout, MO 65726
Email: info@acfacat.com   Fax: (417) 334-5540 Tel: (417) 334-5430

Cat Fanciers Association, Inc. (CFA)
PO Box 1005, Manasquan, NJ 08736-0805
Email: cfa@cfainc.org   Fax: (732) 528-7391 Tel: (732) 528-9797

Cat Fanciers Federation (CFF)
PO Box 661, Gratis, OH 45330
Email: Lalbert933@aol.com Fax: 937-787-4290 Tel: (937) 787-9009

The International Cat Association (TICA)
PO Box 2684, Harlingen, TX 78551
Email: ticaeo@xanadu2.net Tel: (956) 428-8046

GLOSSARY

AACE: American Association of Cat Enthusiasts. A recently formed feline association in America.

ACF: Australian Cat Federation. Major Australian association that represents numerous cat registries.

Agouti: The ticked pattern created by alternate light/dark pigment banding seen along the hairs of a non-mutated cat's coat.

Altered: Cats that have been de-sexed.

ACA: American Cat Association. Oldest of the American registries.

Autosomal: Refers to body cells as opposed to sex (germ) cells.

Awn (bristle) hair: Those hairs that lie between the outer guard hairs of the coat and those that form the undercoat.

Bib: The chest area of the ruff in long and semi-longhaired cats.

Bi-colour: A pattern comprising a colour and white.

Blaze: A marking of colour, usually white, that extends down the nose.

Blood type incompatibility (BTI): Cats have two blood types: *A* and *B*. Type *A* is dominant to type *B* and is the most common. Type *B* mothers should never nurse a type *A* offspring, as this will prove fatal to the kitten.

Break: The area where the nose and forehead meet. Also called the stop.

Breast bone: Sternum.

Britches: The long hair on the back of the hind legs.

Burmese restriction: Refers to the gene that creates the Burmese pattern.

CA: The Cat Association of Britain. A cat registry and the British representative of the FIFe.

Calico: Alternative name for the tortoiseshell and white pattern.

Calling: The unmistakable sound of a female when she is in heat (oestrus) and calling to attract a male.

Cameo: Term given to the red or cream tipped hairs.

Canine teeth: The large paired fangs (dog teeth) of the upper and lower jaw.

Carpus bone: Wrist.

Cat flu: A common name that covers any of the many viruses that affect the respiratory system. Vaccines are available against some of these.

Catnip: Common name for the herb *Nepeta cataria*, whose scent cats find irresistible.

Cat registry: A feline ruling body that issues cat registrations, cat standards and, in general, administrates matters relating to cat show regulations and breed recognition.

Caudal vertebrae: Tail bones.

CCA: Canadian Cat Association. Canada's only feline registry. Administrates in both English and French languages.

CFA: Cat Fanciers Association. The main American registry—the world's largest.

CFF: Cat Fanciers Federation. American cat registry.

CFSA: Cat Federation of Southern Africa.

Champion: In Britain a cat that has won three Challenge Certificates under three different judges, at three different shows. In some countries, such as America, the system may vary and be based on acquiring a specific number of points.

Championship breed status: The final stage in full breed recognition. It can take many years to progress from preliminary to championship status.

Chinchilla: A coat pattern in which only the very tips of the hairs carry pigment, the rest of the hair being white or nearly so.

Chintz: Former name used in Britain for the tortoiseshell and white pattern.

Chromosome: One of paired thread-like structures found in the nucleus of all cells. They contain the genes that collectively determine all aspects of the cat.

Cleft Palate: A birth defect in which the bones of the hard palate do not develop correctly.

Cobby: A compact and sturdily built body.

Colostrum: The milk released by a female for two or three days after a kitten is born and which is rich in antibodies and protein.

Colourpoint: Terms used for the Siamese pattern when seen in other breeds.

Conformation: The way a cat's anatomy is arranged including its coat type, colour and overall appearance.

Congenital: Present from birth.

Counter conditioning: A psychological term for any stimuli that will weaken, stop or replace a given behavioural action.

Cystitis: Inflammation of the bladder caused by bacteria.

Dental formula: The number and type of teeth in a cat. *Adult:* I 3/3 C 1/1 PM 3/2 M 1/1= half jaw (upper/lower) x 2 = 30 *Kitten:* Same as adult, and deciduous, but no molars = 26

Dewclaw: The short toe and claw found on the inside of the front legs above the toes.

Dermatitis: Any of the various skin disorders often commonly called eczema.

Diarrhoea: Common term applied to the semi-liquid state of faecal matter that is the outward indicator of many internal disorders and diseases.

Digitigrade: Walking on the toes like a cat, as opposed to the feet (plantigrade) as in bears and man, or on the nails as in horses (unguiligrade).

Dominant gene: A mutant gene that needs to be present only in single dose to visually express itself.

Double coat: The presence of an obvious topcoat and a softer and dense underfur or coat.

Down hair: The short and soft hairs that create the heat retaining undercoat of a cat's fur.

Entire: A cat that still has its reproductive organs in tact. An unaltered cat.

GLOSSARY

Fading kitten syndrome: The condition where kittens die for no apparent reason, but often because of blood type incompatibility.

Feline calici virus (FCV): Respiratory disorder. A vaccine is available.

Feline dysautonomia: A rare disease of the nervous system also known as Key-Gaskell Syndrome. Permanently dilated pupils are amongst the indicators.

Feline immuno-deficiency virus (FIV): A disease of the white blood cells. No vaccine available.

Feline infectious anaemia (FIA): Disease caused by blood cell parasites transmitted by fleas and ticks.

Feline infectious enteritis (FIE): Disease of the digestive and blood systems. A vaccine is available. Also known as Feline panleukopenia.

Feline infectious peritonitis (FIP): Disease of the digestive and nervous systems: No vaccine available.

Feline leukaemia virus (FeLV): Highly infectious viral disease of the blood system. A vaccine is available.

Feline viral rhinotracheitis (FVR): Respiratory disorder, usually more serious than FCV. A vaccine is available.

Feline urological syndrome (FUS): The feline term for urolithiasis, a condition in which crystals form in the urinary tract.

Felis catus: Scientific name for the domestic cat.

Femur: Thigh bone.

FIFe: Federation Internationale Feline. A world federation of cat associations whose members apply common rules and regulations.

Flank: The area between the ribs and hips of a cat.

Foreign: Cats of a slim or lithe conformation. A group of such cats is in the classification of the GCCF.

GCCF: Governing Council of the Cat Fancy. Britain's largest, and the world's oldest, cat registry.

Gene: The unit of inheritance.

Genotype: The genetic make-up of one or more characteristics.

Gestation period: The time lapse between fertilisation and the birth of kittens, typically 63 days.

Gingivitis: A disease of the gums that results in bad breath, bad teeth and other maladies.

Ground colour: The basic colour in the tabby over which the pattern itself is superimposed.

Guard hairs: The stiff, coarse and long hairs that provide the outer protection to a cat's coat.

Haematoma: Blood blister in cats often found in the ear flap.

Heartbeat rate: In cats this should be 160-240 per minute.

Hereditary myopathy: A condition that negatively affects the muscles, causing problems in head carriage and walking difficulties.

Heterozygous: When each gene of a pair is for different expressions: non-pure-breeding for a given characteristic.

Himalayan: An alternative name for the colourpoint pattern in the Persian breed. In some American associations, it is regarded as a separate breed as the Persian.

Hip dysplasia: Disease of the hip characterised by excessive movement of the femoral head. Usually associated with the larger and heavier breeds.

Hock (ankle): Tarsus bone—the joint that receives the tibia or shin bone.

Homozygous: When both genes of a pair are of for the same expression: pure-breeding for a given characteristic.

Incisor teeth: The six small teeth situated between the canine teeth of each jaw.

Iris: The coloured area that surrounds the eye pupil.

Jacobson's organ: A highly sensitive organ situated in the roof of the mouth and which analyses tastes and smells. Associated with Flehming when cats, usually males, lift their upper lip to receive female scents.

Kitten: For show purposes in Britain a cat that is 14 or more weeks of age but under 9 months of age. In America the age is 16 weeks but under 8 months of age.

Locus: Genetic term for a gene's location along a chromosome (pl. loci).

Masking: Genetic term meaning the ability of a gene to suppress the effect of one or more other genes so that they are not visually apparent. The genetic name for this is epistasis.

Metacarpus bones: Front feet or paw.

Metatarsus bones: Hind feet or paw.

Milk fever (lactational tetany): Condition created in a nursing female through lack of blood calcium levels. Causes staggering and vomiting.

Moggie (Moggy): The old and still popular common name for a mongrel cat.

Molar teeth: The teeth behind the premolars.

Mutation: The change in the way a gene expresses itself visually or in its physiological functioning.

Muzzle: The jaws and mouth.

Neck bones: Cervical vertebrae.

Neuter class: A show class for cats that have been de-sexed.

Neutering: De-sexing. Castration in males—removal of testes. Spaying in females—removal of uterus and ovaries

Odd-eyed: White cats having one blue- and one orange-coloured eye.

pH value: A number used to denote the degree of acidity or alkalinity of a solution, neutral being seven. Values below this are acidic, above this alkaline. Cats require a urine pH of about 6 or just below this.

Pedigree: A document that indicates the line of descent. A moggie may have a pedigree as well as a pure-bred cat.

Pen (cage) judging: When cats are judged immediately outside their holding pen or cage.

GLOSSARY

Pet passport: A document that allows a cat to travel to and from Britain within the European Community without the need to be quarantined on its entry or return.

Pewter: A tipped pattern similar to the shaded silver, but where the eye colour is orange or copper, not green.

Phenotype: The visual expression of a gene—its appearance, i.e. longhair, rex coat, colour, pattern, etc.

Plasmocytic-lymphocytic stomatitis: Gingivitis, a gum disease.

Polydactyl: Having more than five toes on the front feet (including the dewclaw) and four on the hind feet.

Polygenic: When any given characteristic is determined by a number of genes rather than a pair.

Preliminary Breed Status: The first stage towards full breed recognition with the GCCF and other registries.

Premier: In cat shows the neutered cat's title, equivalent of a champion.

Premolars: The teeth behind the canine and in front of the molars.

Prepotent: Said of a cat of either sex that is able to consistently pass its type to its offspring, regardless of its mate's type. This is usually due to homozygosity of genotype.

Prolapse: A condition in which the uterus or rectum is pushed out of the body due to excess straining.

Provisional breed status: The second stage towards full breed recognition by the GCCF and some other registries.

Pulse rate: In cats this should be 160-240 per minute.

Pupil: The dark-coloured centre of the eye.

Queen: An unaltered female cat.

Quick: That part of the nail that contains a blood vessel.

Registration certificate: A document that records the birth date of a kitten, its immediate ancestry, and its breeder and owner.

Reinforcement: A psychological term for any external or internal stimuli that will encourage retention of any given action.

Recessive gene: A mutant gene that must be present in double dose before it is expressed visually.

Respiration rate: In cats this should be 20-30 per minute.

Ring judging: When cats are taken from their pens to be judged on a table.

Ringworm: A fungal infection of the skin.

Self-colour: A colour that is the same all over the body.

Sex chromosomes: Paired chromosomes of unequal length. One is designated as *X* while the shorter one is the *Y*. In mammals the male is *XY* and the female *XX*.

Sex-linked: Any trait found on the sex chromosomes and which link the sex to the trait. The colour red and its dilution, cream, are sex-linked colours and carried on the *X* chromosome.

Shaded: Tipped coat pattern midway between the chinchilla and the smoke.

Shoulder bone: Scapula.

Siamese restriction: Refers to the gene that creates the Siamese (colourpoint) coat pattern.

Smoke: Darkest of the tipped coat patterns.

Squint: When the eyes appear to be permanently looking at the nose—cross-eyed.

Sternum: Breastbone.

Stress: Subconscious fear or nervousness often difficult to identify. It reduces the effectiveness of the immune system and induces illness more rapidly, while slowing down recovery.

Tail bones: Caudal vertebrae.

Tarsus bone: Hock or ankle.

Taurine: An essential amino acid that can cause blindness in cats if it is deficient in the diet.

Temperature: The normal temperature for a healthy cat is between 38–39° C (100—102° F).

Thigh bone: Femur.

Third eyelid: Also known as the haw or nictitating membrane. Located in the corner of the eye, it is usually only seen clearly when the cat is unwell.

Threshold: A psychological term for the degree of stimulus required to elicit a response. A low threshold requires minimal stimulus.

TICA: The International Cat Association. One of the larger American registries.

TCA: Traditional Cat Association. American registry formed to cater to those wishing to preserve traditional forms of breeds such as the Persian and Siamese.

Tom: An unaltered male cat.

Trichobezoar: In veterinary language, this means hairballs.

Tri-colour: An alternative name for the tortoiseshell and white. A three-colour pattern comprising two pigment colours and white.

Vetting in: The veterinary examination of each cat before it is allowed into a show venue. Not always a requirement outside the UK.

WCF: World Cat Federation. German-based organisation with member registries in a few other countries, notably Brazil.

Whisker break: The area immediately behind the whisker pads.

Zoonoses: Diseases that can be passed between animals and humans.

Zygote: The fertilised egg (ovum) from which the organism will develop.

INDEX

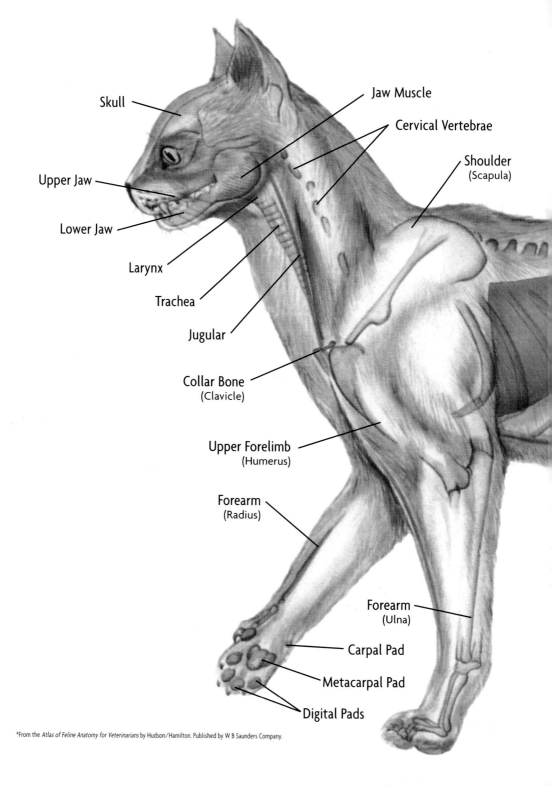

Skull

Jaw Muscle

Cervical Vertebrae

Shoulder
(Scapula)

Upper Jaw

Lower Jaw

Larynx

Trachea

Jugular

Collar Bone
(Clavicle)

Upper Forelimb
(Humerus)

Forearm
(Radius)

Forearm
(Ulna)

Carpal Pad

Metacarpal Pad

Digital Pads

*From the *Atlas of Feline Anatomy for Veterinarians* by Hudson/Hamilton. Published by W B Saunders Company.

THE ANATOMY OF THE CAT

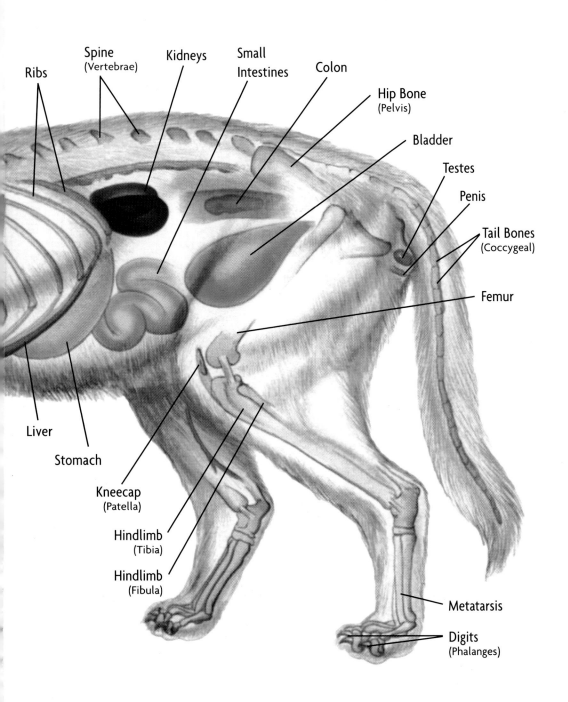

Ribs

Spine
(Vertebrae)

Kidneys

Small
Intestines

Colon

Hip Bone
(Pelvis)

Bladder

Testes

Penis

Tail Bones
(Coccygeal)

Femur

Liver

Stomach

Kneecap
(Patella)

Hindlimb
(Tibia)

Hindlimb
(Fibula)

Metatarsis

Digits
(Phalanges)

My Birman Cat

PUT YOUR KITTEN'S FIRST PICTURE HERE

Kitten's Name _____

Date _____ Photographer _____